Centering
a
Lopsided
Egg

Chap 5 to end
Congruence
Like - dis
Power
Responsiveness

For mon. 10-18

Find illustrations (pictures)
of the ego status. pg 21

Born to _____ pg 24

Centering a Lopsided Egg

Reflections on Communication Balance

ED RINTYE
Grossmont College

Allyn and Bacon, Inc.
Boston · London · Sydney

Library of Congress Cataloging in Publication Data

Rintye, Ed, 1937-
    Centering a lopsided egg.

    1. Communication—Psychological aspects. I. Title.
BF637.C45R56   153   74-23719

ISBN 0-205-04659-2

Second printing . . . July, 1975

ACKNOWLEDGMENTS

Chapter 1

p. 1: photo by John Severson, *Surfer* Magazine photo. p. 2: photos by Talbot Lovering. p. 5: e. e. cummings, "A Poet's Advice to Students," from *E. E. Cummings: A Miscellany,* edited by George Firmage and reprinted by permission of Harcourt Brace Jovanovich, Inc. p. 5: cartoon by Joseph Farris, reproduced by special permission of *Playboy* Magazine; copyright © 1971 by Playboy. p. 7: Richard Bach, *Jonathan Livingston Seagull,* copyright © 1970 by Richard D. Bach, copyright © 1970 by Russell Munson.

Chapter 2

p. 13: Clare Boothe Luce, "What Really Killed Marilyn?" *Life* Magazine, 7 August 1964, pp. 68-78. pp. 14, 15, 19, and 20: United Press International photos. p. 23: article condensed from "Multiple Identity" by Kenneth J. Gergen in *Psychology Today* Magazine, May 1972. Copyright © Communications / Research / Machines, Inc. p. 32: from *Knots* by R. D. Laing. Copyright © 1970 by the R. D. Laing Trust. Reprinted by permission of Pantheon Books, a Division of Random House, Inc., and Associated Book Publishers Ltd. p. 33: Erma Bombeck, "Up the Wall: Husband in Charge," and illustration by Marylin Hafner reprinted by permission from the January 1973 issue of *Good Housekeeping* Magazine, © 1973 by the Hearst

To my soul wife,
teacher,
and
co-creator

Contents

*interpersonal ecology. Healthy relationships do not come in
seed packages, but like a garden effort they do reflect our sense
of balance, harmony, and mutual respect. (Included are "The
Listener," John Berry; "Sucker," Carson McCullers; "A Fuzzy
Tale," Claude Steiner; "Generation Gap," Newsweek; and "Will
You Be My Friend?" James Kavanaugh.)*

4 Being through Symbols 77

*Our need to touch one another is fulfilled through the fragile
tool of language. Unless symbols are used with understanding
and sensitivity, they break down, crack up. Communication can
become a very gooey thing, indeed. (Original material with
illustrations.)*

5 Being without Words 95

*Hundreds of thousands of years of human evolution have given
us sensitivity to many different vocabularies of nonverbal
symbols. Awareness of these in relation to spoken language is
one key to balanced communication. (Readings include "The
Sounds of Silence," Ed and Mildred Hall; "Startling New
Research from the Man Who 'Talks' to Plants," Janice and
Charles Robbins; and "Man's Hidden Environment," David
Dempsey.)*

6 Being Centered 143

*Communication behavior, like all behavior, is a reflection of
personal balance. To achieve human communication is to make
of life an art. (Mostly original material with poetry excerpts
from Ric Masten and Bernard Gunther, and bits and pieces of
Abraham Maslow, Harold Lasswell, and the I Ching.)*

Preface

This is a book about human be-ing through communication.
For people who like to enjoy their reading.
For eggs who find tight boxes uncomfortable.
It is **not** a book of answers.
I am fresh out.
But . . .

> It will stimulate questions;
> it will imply alternatives.

Instructors will find that they can use the book in many different ways to supplement their own approach to studying human interaction through communication.

This is not a text, but a fun book of ramblings and readings that relates to many of the central issues in healthy communing. I hope I have tempted readers to frame their own meaningful questions about these issues.

So *don't* look for answers here.

Look within yourself for those.

Here you will find a lot of high-interest material, often contradictory, certainly contrasting. You will find many different biases, and no pretense by me of "objectivity." I don't believe it ever truly exists.

I feel the title of this book suggests the direction of my personal interest. I very much see myself as an egg, with all of the pulsating rhythm and potential you share. We all share.

And centering that potential is my passion.

I have assumed throughout that all behavior communicates, and that behavior reflects personal balance. The question of balance or centering is basic, then, when I think about improving my communing.

My editor thinks you might like to know something about me, besides what you will read between the lines in the pages that follow.

So . . . o.k.

I'm thirty-seven years wrinkled. Enthusiastically married. Enjoy natural food and imaginative sex. Have slight back trouble due to spine curve. I've worked as a short-order cook, night club magician, journalist, fruit peddler, rent-a-cop, carnival pitchman, military trooper and officer, and teacher. I also remember selling seed packets door to door in order to earn a Red Ryder BB gun. Never sold enough, though.

Currently my interests include organic gardening, human growth therapies, esp research, nonverbal communication, raising sane children, and keeping neighborhood dogs and cats out of my garden.

My most meaningful activity is my family life.

We work at it, play with it, joy and pain through it, and learn together. Son Kahlil, daughter Paulyn, mothers Paula and Lyn, brother Dan, and in-laws/grampas Norine, Joey, Ted, and Von. George, Larry, and Polly have left us, but still reach over from time to time.

My most meaningful relationship now is with Paula, to whom I am appreciatively married and from whom has flowed much creative editing of this book. She is one of those rare people who have the ability to make of family living an art form. Right now she is engrossed in being a mother. Tomorrow, who knows?

Naturally I owe special thanks to special people.

Holly for her egg energy.

Lyn for the Fuzzies.

Nancy McJennett (the book designer), Malinda Cowles (the illustrator), and Sheryl Avruch (the production editor) for their creative and energetic involvement.

And Frank Ruggirello, my editor, for his sensitivity, competence, and nesting instincts.

Introduction

Have you ever pondered the miracle of balance?

I think of myself as a kid walking fence tops; that's one kind of balance I counted on to get me home by the quickest route after mom had yelled "supper" for the third time.

And seeing Olympic divers twisting and turning around their centers of gravity, entering the water without a splash.

And feeling when my clay is centered on the wheel so I can raise a pot without it becoming lopsided and falling over, ploop.

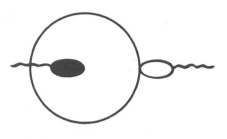

One experience with balance we've all shared. Remember?

When you combined two parts to create a more fertile egg/you.

From that centered place you were wonderfully creative and perfectly balanced. Remember how easily you balanced nutrition demands, balanced body growth, nothing too fast or too slow? You knew your plan and schedule; you directed the action. And when you were ready, you began human be-ing.

That was a ponderful bit of balancing.

Ponderful and wonderful.

Robert Browning said it this way:

There is an inmost center in us all

Where truth abides in fulness . . .

And "to know" consists rather in

Opening out a way whence the imprisoned splendour

May escape.

Many psychologists believe it is natural throughout our *entire life-span* to retain this sensitivity to our own inner being: the sense for balanced living.

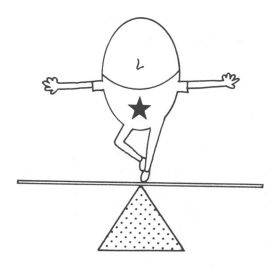

Dr. Carl Rogers, for example, has observed that when a person is in touch with his organismic center he tends to act in ways that enhance his own life and the lives of the people around him. Such a person lives by his own internal values rather than by the values of his neighbors or of society. Abraham Maslow calls such people "self-actualized." M. C. Richards refers to them as "on center."

I call them rare.

Let's be honest . . .

HOW MANY PEOPLE LIKE THIS DO YOU KNOW?

Mom?

Dad?

Teachers?

Anybody?

4   Somewhere between birth and **NOW** I lost my balance, moved "off center." Became lopsided.

HOW ABOUT YOU?

In wondering "What happened?" I notice that my society actually *rewards* me for being lopsided! All I have to do is to think and behave as expected by others. Play a kind of fitting game. Soon I am known to be a "good" egg, and rewards follow.

REWARDS FOR "GOOD" EGGS

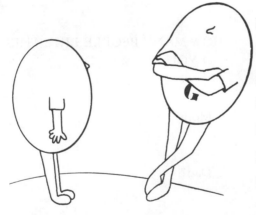

PARENTAL LOVE

HIGH GRADES

EMPLOYMENT

SOCIAL ACCEPTANCE

PUBLIC OFFICE

MILITARY HONORS

POWER OVER OTHERS

YOU NAME IT

This process is called "socialization," except by such people as poet e. e. cummings, who wrote:

"To be nobody-but-yourself in a world which is doing its best, night and day, to make you everybody else—means to fight the hardest battle which any human being can fight, and never stop fighting."

KNOW WHAT HE MEANS?

I think this was what tempted me from awareness, encouraged me away from reliance on my own inner knowing. I lost sight of my self and was carried away by the process, as the cartoon suggests.

Once I bit into the cultural apple, I turned to *others* to tell me what to value, how to view my self, proper measures of "worth," how to view other people, and ways I could and could not live/relate/communicate.

Of course, all cultures train their young in this way. Our culture is neither unique nor "wrong" just because it

"Don't let go—he's a rare one."

selectively rewards certain attitudes and behaviors. In fact, it could be said that to some degree this training gives me some comparison and contrast material I need to define my identity.

SO WHAT'S THE HARM?

The harm is that I tend to forget that *I* am in charge of my life. If I give up inner judgment, inner response, and rely only upon external cultural norms to guide my life, I greatly restrict my exploration and my potential. Socialization is little more than training in acceptance of my culture's rules of behavior. After many years of such conditioning and public evaluation of my "progress" (schools), I may reach a point of such amnesia that I am deemed "responsible." Nothing could be further from the truth.

In my view, I can be "response-able" only when I am organismically present and *able* to *respond* from my inner core. This involves much more than the simple imitative process of playing out other people's expectations in the correct manner. To be able to respond to life means to me to be open and flowing from my conscious center, to move with experience. From the center of the wheel, many spokes ray out. My center has 360 degrees of vision and possible response. Full circle of potential. *This,* to me, is being response-able.

HAVE YOU EVER MET AN UP-TIGHT DAISY?

Flowers never forget who they are.

They have organismic balance.

Perception and response from internal center.

This does not mean that I must reveal my center response/knowing completely to others. I have choice to share or not. But *I* must be in touch with that fulcrum point of my being.

I lose my balance and distort my communication when I limit my perception and response solely to cultural "shoulds" and "oughts."

To the degree that I claim for myself the internal and external freedom to flow with *all* of life, to that degree I may achieve balanced communication.

"Come along then," said Jonathan. "Climb with me away from the ground, and we'll begin."

"You don't understand. My wing. I can't move my wing."

"Maynard Gull, you have the freedom to be yourself, your true self, here and now, and nothing can stand in your way. It is the Law of the Great Gull, the Law that is."

"Are you saying that I can fly?"

"I say you are free."

As simply and as quickly as that, Kirk Maynard Gull spread his wings, effortlessly, and lifted into the dark night air. The Flock was aroused from sleep by his cry, as loud as he could scream it, from five hundred feet up; "*I can fly! Listen! I CAN FLY!*"

By sunrise there were nearly a

8 thousand birds standing outside the circle of students, looking curiously at Maynard. They didn't care whether they were seen or not, and they listened, trying to understand Jonathan Seagull.

He spoke of very simple things— that it is right for a gull to fly, that freedom is the very nature of his being, that whatever stands against that freedom must be set aside, be it ritual or superstition or limitation in any form.

"Set aside," came a voice from the multitude, "even if it be the Law of the Flock?"

"The only true law is that which leads to freedom," Jonathan said. "There is no other."

"How do you expect us to fly as you fly?" came another voice. "You are special and gifted and divine, above other birds."

"Look at Fletcher! Lowell! Charles-Roland! Judy Lee! Are they also special and gifted and divine? No more than you are, no more than I am. They only difference, the very only one, is that they have begun to understand what they really are and have begun to practice it."

RICHARD BACH
Jonathan Livingston Seagull

In other words, communication is being you.
Your way.
And being understood by those who genuinely want to hear.

2

Being
My
"Self"

All right, then.

Balanced communication is the ebb and flow of perception and response. A natural tide of harmonizing rhythms between me and my listener.

And all I need do to stay in touch with this tide is to be still, and keep my self open. That's all. That's All.

BUT...

For me to remain aware of this flow, conscious of this process, means that I must KNOW MY "SELF."

10   I mean, if my "self" is the starting point, my reference point in perception and response, then it follows that:

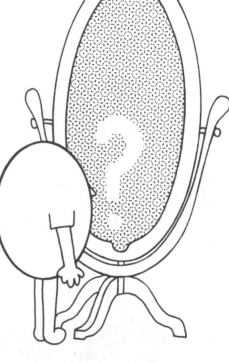

WHO I AM
shapes

HOW I COMMUNICATE

WHAT I COMMUNICATE

WHEN I COMMUNICATE

WHERE I COMMUNICATE

WITH WHOM AND *WHETHER*.

Trying to understand my communication behavior—without understanding my self—is like trying to perceive an iceberg by looking only at the tip above the water line.

*The way I see my
"self" filters and shapes
my perception and response.*

So you and I must face a fundamental question: What is a "self"? *Your* self, for example.

Go on. Close this book for a minute.
Describe your self. Who are you?

How did you answer?

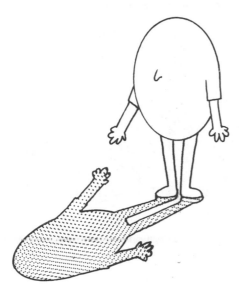

By the job you do?

By what others say?

By your physical form?

By your group memberships?

By your credit cards?

By learned religious doctrine?

All of the above?

*Shadow, shadow, whom
I see,
Are you you?
Or are you me?*

None of the above?

Ignored the question?

Some behavioral scientists in our culture answer this question by speaking of a person's "self-concept." This popular idea suggests that early in life each of us forms a mental picture of the world and his place in it. The growing child uses as "information mirrors" his parents, other kids, babysitters, teachers, the television set, and so on. With what data he receives about himself from others, he organizes a firm concept of self. This looking glass identity tag includes his self-worth, lovability, competence, power, body form and beauty, and sexuality.

Formed at a very early age, this self-image seems hard to change later in adult life.

12 An old saying expresses it well: "As the twig is bent, so grows the tree."

WHAT DO YOU THINK ABOUT THIS APPROACH TO "SELF"?

One painful implication is that as growing young Eggs, we might be the unaware victims of distorted, cracked, or shattered mirrors around us. If the reflections we build on in our childhood years mirror us as unloved, unloving, unworthy, powerless, incompetent, or ugly, then the self-concept we create may be warped, indeed. In this sense, the sins of the parents *are* visited upon the children.

IT IS
POSSIBLE
THAT MUCH
ADULT
PROBLEM
BEHAVIOR
IS LITTLE
MORE THAN
THE ACTING
OUT OF
POOR
SELF-CONCEPTS
FORMED
DURING
CHILDHOOD

Fortunate is the young Egg who grows in the warmth of reflected lovingness, worthiness, power, competence, and beauty. Mirrors of such true quality are uncommon, but their impact is great. Centered Eggs are found most often in such nests.

WHAT DID YOUR EARLY MIRRORS TELL YOU? AND NOW?

For your contemplation I want to share a "case study" that illustrates this approach to self-concept. The story is of the growth and development of a beautiful Egg named Norma Jeane Mortenson.

As you learn of the mirrors that shaped young Norma Jeane, perhaps you will understand better her adult life and death as a Hollywood star . . . known to the public as Marilyn Monroe.

what Really killed marilyn?

BY CLARE BOOTHE LUCE

Early on Sunday morning, Aug. 5, 1962, Marilyn Monroe died by her own hand. The suicide of this radiant woman, "The Love Goddess of the Nuclear Age," was splashed across the front pages of the world and produced an orgy of public commentary . . . obsessed by the question of why this woman, possessing beauty, fame and money in abundance, had so feared or hated life that she could no longer face it.

. . . although views differed as to who or what had condemned and finally executed her, Hollywood was far and away the most favored villain. The *New York Daily Worker* indicted the capitalistic motion picture producers who "turn woman into a piece of meat" and sell not only their bodies but the "souls of their fellow human beings." Britain's *Manchester Guardian* saw her as the victim of her fans, forever haunted by "a nightmare of herself 60 feet tall and naked before the howling mob." The *New York Times* blamed the Hollywood star system.

. . . perhaps what most wants saying is that whoever or whatever killed Marilyn it was *not* Hollywood.

Indeed, the "howling mob" who made her see herself as "60 feet tall and naked" gave her the only form of sustained emotional security she ever knew, or perhaps was capable of understanding.

A few weeks before she died Marilyn told *Life:* "I think that sexuality is only attractive when it's natural. . . . We are all born sexual creatures, thank God, but it's a pity so many people despise and crush this natural gift . . . if I'm going to be a symbol of something, I'd rather have it sex. . . ."

Whatever else Marilyn had hoped —and failed—to find in life, her "howling" public must have been what she most feared to lose when she reached for her last and lethal dose of barbiturates. Surely she realized that the mob worship of her for her pure sexuality could not last more than a few years longer. Breasts, belly, bottom must one day sag. She was 36, and her mirror had begun to warn her.

A girl entering her teens, especially an American girl, has intense, often lengthy encounters with a looking glass. She learns early that the male has a natural preference for young and pretty women. But too often she continues even after marriage and motherhood to believe that *who* she is is *what* she looks like in the mirror. Advertising spends billions of dollars fostering this essentially immature attitude in adult women. For, the more mature and emotionally secure a woman becomes the less she turns to the looking glass to give her self-confidence and a sense of her own personhood, and the more she looks into the eyes of the people she loves and who love her for the true reflection of her identity.

Too often the American woman believes what the advertising industry tells her she is or should be.

After Marilyn passed 30, her sessions with her studio mirror must have been increasingly agonizing experiences. The growing hostility and aggressiveness she began to show in her later years, especially to men who worked with her, and the endless changes of clothes and protracted primpings in her dressing room, the fits of vomiting just before the cameras began to grind—all these may have foreshadowed her terror of that hour when her multiple lover, the wolf-whistling mobs of men and oohing and aahing women would desert her.

What, then, would make her valuable, even in her own eyes? Who was Marilyn Monroe if not that lovely girl on the screen, that delectable creature she saw in the mirror?

She knew who the "real me" was. But this was an admission she sought to escape . . . one of the saddest and most frightened little girls ever born—Norma Jeane Mortenson.

Her mother, Mrs. Gladys Baker, was a pretty, red-haired 24-year-old woman who worked as a film cutter for RKO. Mrs. Baker's father and mother had been in mental institutions and a brother had committed suicide. She had married Baker when she was 15, and borne him two children. He deserted her a few years later, taking his children with him. A succession of men followed him in Mrs. Baker's bed, including one Edward Mortenson, an itinerant bread-baker. The child of this casual union was born on June 1, 1926, in Los Angeles, and baptized Norma Jeane Mortenson. The father was not present: he disappeared, and forever, the day Gladys Baker told him that she was pregnant.

Following the birth of her child, Gladys Baker returned to her job. In her moody and feckless fashion, she cared for Norma Jeane during the first few years of her infancy. Then she began to give evidence of violent mental disturbance and was committed to an institution. Norma Jeane was made a ward of the County of Los Angeles. For the next four or five years she was farmed out by the County Welfare Agency to a series of foster parents, who were paid $20 a month. None of her foster homes

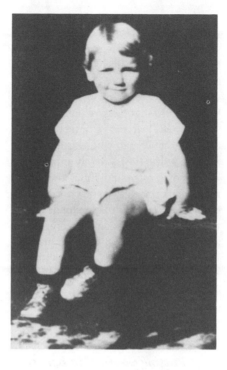

apparently offered her even the barest security, much less love. The pattern of anxiety, hostility and moral confusion that underlay all Marilyn's human relations in later life was indelibly set in these early childhood years. "I always felt insecure and in the way," she once said, "but most of all I felt scared. . . . I guess I wanted love more than anything in the world."

Have you ever felt this way?

At the age of 7 or 8, in one of these "homes," Norma Jeane was seduced by an elderly star boarder. She recalled in later years that he was an old man who wore a heavy golden watch chain over the wide expanse of his vest, and that he gave her a nickel "not to tell." When she nevertheless did tell, the woman who was her foster mother at the time severely punished her for making up lies about the "fine man." The unhealthy and confused emotional correlations she made all through her life among sex, money, and guilt may have stemmed in part from this ugly first encounter with man's lust. After the punishment she suffered for the rape of her innocence, she acquired a stammer which remained with her throughout her life.

turning point of her life.

also

> *Putting yourself in her place, can you understand her response?*

Norma Jeane, like millions of other small girls, also dreamed of becoming a movie star. But Norma Jeane had a special gift. It began to manifest itself when she was 12. One morning, before going to school, she decided to put on lipstick, eyebrow pencil and a borrowed blue sweater one size too small for her. "My arrival in school started everyone buzzing," she recalled. "The boys began screaming and groaning. . . . Even the girls paid a little attention to me." Norma Jeane discovered, to her delight, the one dazzling gift that had been bestowed on her at birth—an exuberant, vital, almost atomic capacity to project her sexuality. Marilyn Monroe was in the making.

What Marilyn's sex life was like in the days before she sought to storm the golden gates of Hollywood can only be surmised. It cannot, even by today's easy standards, have been "moral." For she had no father or mother image to guide her as to the proper behavior of boys and girls. Never having known the face of maternal or even fraternal love, she was certainly incapable of giving what she herself had never known. . . . Marilyn offered this explanation: "I guess I was soured on marriage because all I knew was men who swore at their wives, and fathers who never played with their kids. The husbands I remember from my childhood got drunk regularly, and the wives were always drab women who never had a chance to dress or make up or be taken anywhere to have fun. I grew up thinking, 'If this is marriage, who needs it?' "

Despising marriage, deeply distrustful of both men and women but nevertheless hungry to the core of her being for admiration, affection, and acceptance as a person, she sought "love" with what must have been a fever-pitch promiscuity. Indeed, by the time she was entering womanhood a miracle was needed to save her from a life of overt or covert prostitution.

That miracle happened. Its name was Hollywood.

In 1945 she found employment with The Blue Books Model Agency in Los Angeles as a photographers' model. The agency advised her to dye her dark blonde hair a golden blonde. Within a year her face, ringed with golden curls—and great peachy reaches of her body—had become familiar and welcome items in all the men's magazines from *Laff* to *Pic*. Soon a screen test was arranged for her and she was signed by 20th Century-Fox.

Marilyn's first big movie break came . . . in *The Asphalt Jungle*. It called for an angel-faced blonde with a wickedly curvaceous figure. Marilyn was tested for the part, and on neither score was she found wanting.

Her part in *The Asphalt Jungle* got her movie career onto the ways. But . . . it should be remembered the picture that first made her famous had nothing to do with the movies. It was a photograph of Marilyn in the nude, for which she had cheerfully posed when she was modeling. . . .

Asked, years after the shot had been circulated world-wide, what she had on when she posed for it, she replied, "The radio."

The story of Marilyn's years as the Love Goddess is too well known to need repeating. But behind the facade of the gay and happy star, this "basic girl," the tragic Lolita, remained unchanged and unchangeable.

Do you believe anyone is "unchangeable"?

A year and a half after Marilyn's suicide, the question of "Who killed our Marilyn?" was unexpectedly revived by a competent witness—her third husband, playwright Arthur Miller. In his autobiographical and self-defensive play, *After the Fall* . . . Miller, not surprisingly, finds that whoever else was "responsible" for Marilyn's death, it certainly was *not* Arthur Miller. But neither does Miller blame Hollywood. He holds that Marilyn wrought her own destruction by insisting on seeing herself as the utterly helpless victim of her parents, her lovers and husbands, her profession and her friends—a victim who, in her own eyes, could be "saved" only by a "limitless love."

[Miller] encouraged her to seek psychiatric help and to bolster her self-esteem by developing whatever gifts she believed she might have as an actress.

Hollywood's reactions to Marilyn's latter-day dramatic aspirations were cruel. One producer voiced this judgment on her dramatic chances: "Act? That blonde can't act her way out of a Whirl-pool bra!" Mike Todd called her "the greatest con artist of them all." And Billy Wilder, who was her director in *Some Like It Hot*, and one of the few in Hollywood she respected, was quoted: "The question is whether Marilyn is a person at all, or one of the greatest DuPont products ever invented. She has breasts like granite, and a brain like Swiss cheese, full of holes."

Perhaps these judgments on Marilyn's dramatic talents were as false as they were harsh. But it was certainly true that Marilyn did not have the self-control or self-discipline to become a Broadway dramatic star.

Marilyn died, really, on a Saturday night. The girl whose translucent beauty had made her the "love object" of millions of unknown lonely or unsatisfied males had no date that evening.

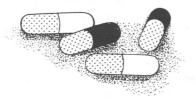

Apparently none of the men or women she knew well had, in the end, cared enough for her to "hang around" and try to cheer her up, although everyone knew she was suffering, physically and mentally. And Marilyn evidently neither loved nor trusted anyone enough to seek help.

Above all, Marilyn was profoundly suspicious of the motives of everyone in her own regard. It was why she walked like a cat, alone, in the midnight alleys of her soul, rejecting lovers and friends before they could get around—as her mother and all her foster parents had done—to rejecting her.

She had an almost psychopathic fear of being "used"; financially used as she had first been by foster parents who tolerated her only because she brought in her $20 board money; sexually used, as by the man who gave her a nickel for the first display of her sex; professionally used, as in the nature of their business, by producers and agents.

In the play *After the Fall* Miller makes her say, "I'm a joke that brings in money." Marilyn would consider it the cream of the jest that, even after her death, the joke is still a big money-maker. For when Hollywood is done with *After the Fall*, Marilyn's ghostly ears will once again hear the music she loved best—the loud, lusty masculine wolf whistles of her adoring public.

For all its corn, the simplest lesson of Marilyn's life is that children need parents, or parent substitutes, who not only love them but who love and respect one another. Without this greatest of all cradle gifts, a happy home, it is all but impossible for them in adulthood to deal with either of those two imposters—failure or success.

The suicide rate in Los Angeles County jumped 40% during the three weeks of "hot" publicity given her death.

rejecting lovers and friends before they could get around—as her mother and all her foster parents had done—to rejecting her.

20 Cinderella lives happily ever after only in the fairy tale. In real life, no matter how many clothes she puts on—or takes off—her heart remains embittered and her spirit soiled by the ashes she swept in childhood.

After reading this article on Marilyn Monroe, I found myself with this question:

IS IT POSSIBLE FOR AN ADULT
TO CHANGE THE WAY HE SEES
HIMSELF?

Mrs. Luce, who wrote the article, seems to believe that once a self-concept is formed in early childhood, people find it "almost impossible" to change their view of themselves. If she is right, there are implications here for those of us who want to change our communication behaviors.

WHAT ARE SOME IMPLICATIONS YOU SEE?

Marilyn Monroe serves me a good example as I try to consider the connection between communication behavior and a person's self-concept. In her case, do you see any connection? And what about *your* case?

Did you notice . . .

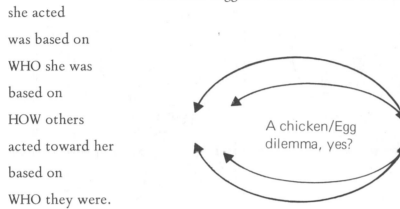

This article suggests of Ms. Monroe's life that HOW
she acted

was based on

WHO she was

based on

HOW others

acted toward her

based on

WHO they were.

A chicken/Egg dilemma, yes?

In fact, this is the rhythmic ebb and flow of perception and response between people of which I spoke earlier in the chapter.

Defined in this way, communication is made up of the WHO's and the HOW's of daily life. And that is why we now continue our investigation of the WHO . . . that is, the "self."

Psychologist Kenneth Gergen has a different approach to identity than self-concept. He believes in multiple identity. I find it expanding to compare and contrast his view with the first one we've considered. You might enjoy the same trip.

R

S(Encoding   Channel   (Decoding

SUPEREGG

THE HEALTHY, HAPPY HUMAN BEING WEARS MANY MASKS

Polonius undoubtedly had good intentions; his counsel to his son seems eminently reasonable. It has a ring of validity and it fits our religious and moral values. But it is poor psychology. I think we are not apt to find a single, basic self to which we can be true.

This above all,—to thine own self be true;
And it must follow, as the night the day,
Thou canst not then be false to any man.

HAMLET, Act 1, Scene 3

I came to this belief after writing letters to close friends one evening. When I read over what I had written, I was first surprised, then alarmed. I came across as a completely different person in each letter: in one, I was morose, pouring out a philosophy of existential sorrow; in another I was a lusty realist; in a third I was a light-hearted jokester; and so on.

I had felt completely honest and authentic as I wrote each letter; at no time was I aware of putting on a particular style to please or impress a particular friend. And yet, a stranger reading those letters all together would have no idea who I am. This realization staggered me. Which letter, if any, portrayed the true me? Was there such

Condensed from "Multiple Identity" by Kenneth J. Gergen, *Psychology Today* (May 1972).

an entity—or was I simply a chameleon, reflecting others' views of me?

PARCELS. Such questions I find are widespread in our culture. One young woman described the problem to her encounter group thus: "I feel like I'm contradictory . . . and people keep hitting me with the you're-not-what-you-seem issue, and it's really wearing me down . . . it's like I feel I can only give part here to one person and part there to another, but then I become a bunch of parcels. If I could just get all my reactions together. . . ."

Her difficulties evoke Erik Erikson's classical description of identity diffusion: a state of bewilderment, typical of the young, at the lack of a firm sense of self. Other psychiatrists speak of self-alienation, a depressed feeling of estrangement from the masks of identity that society forces on the individual. Contemporary critics argue that rapid social and technological upheaval has created a crisis of identity: an individual no longer can develop and maintain a strong, integrated sense of personal identity. Writers from Alexander Pope to sociologist Erving Goffman have been alternately impressed and irritated at the use of masks in social life.

BASES. Such critics and psychologists have been working on two assumptions:

(1) that it is *normal* for a person to develop a firm and coherent sense of identity, and

(2) that it is *good* and healthy for him to do so, and pathological not to.

The first assumption underlies virtually all psychological research on the development of the self. Psychologists maintain that the child learns to identify himself positively (high self-esteem) or negatively (the inferiority complex); they have sought the origins of such feelings in different kinds of home environments and socialization styles. They believe that once the sense of self is fixed, it remains a stable feature of personality. Moreover, knowing a person's fixed level of self-esteem allows us to predict his actions; his neurotic or healthy behavior, his assertiveness in social relations, his academic performance, his generosity, and more.

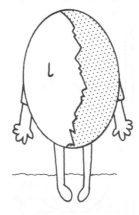

The second assumption—that a unified sense of self is good and that inconsistency is bad—is so pervasive in our cultural traditions that it is virtually unquestioned. At the turn of the century William James said that the person with a divided sense of self had a "sick soul": he was to be pitied and redeemed. The psychologist Prescott Lecky argued that inconsistency of self was the very basis of neurotic behavior. And of course we are all apt to applaud the person of firm character who has self-integrity: we think of the inconsistent person as wishy-washy, undependable, a fake.

DOUBT. My research over the past few years has led me to question both of these assumptions very seriously. I doubt that a person normally develops a coherent sense of identity, and to the extent that he does, he may experience severe emotional distress.

Our studies dealt with

> THE INFLUENCE OF THE "OTHER"
> THE SITUATION
> THE INDIVIDUAL'S MOTIVES

In each experiment, we would vary one of these three factors, holding the others constant. We would thus assess their impact on the subject's presentation of himself; and when the whole procedure was over, we explored the participant's feelings of self-alienation and sincerity.

SELVES. William James believed that one's close friends mold his public identity: "A man has as many differ-

---

> *I doubt that a person normally develops a coherent sense of identity.*

The long-term intimate relationship, so cherished in our society, is an unsuspected cause of this distress because it freezes and constricts identity.

My colleagues and I designed a series of studies to explore the shifting masks of identity, hoping to document the shifts in an empirically reliable way. We wanted to find the factors that influence the individual's choice of masks; we were interested in both outward appearances and inward feelings of personal identity. To what extent are we changeable, and in what condition are we most likely to change? Do alterations in public identity create a nagging sense of self-alienation? How do we reconcile social role-playing with a unified personality?

ent social selves as there are distinct groups of persons about whose opinion he cares." Our research supports this hypothesis, and goes further. ONE'S IDENTITY WILL CHANGE MARKEDLY EVEN IN THE PRESENCE OF STRANGERS.

In an experiment at the University of Michigan, Stanley J. Morse and I sought male applicants for an interesting summer job that paid well. As each volunteer reported in, we seated him alone in a room with a long table, and gave him a battery of tests to fill out. Among them, of course, was a self-evaluation questionnaire. We explained that his responses on this questionnaire would have nothing to do with his chances of being hired, but that we needed his honest answers to construct a good test. As the applicant sat there working, we sent in a stooge—supposedly another applicant for the job.

STOOGES. In half of the cases, the stooge was our Mr. Clean. He was a striking figure: well-tailored business suit, gleaming shoes, and a smart attaché case, from which he took a dozen sharpened pencils and a book of Plato. The other half of the job applicants met our Mr. Dirty, who arrived with a torn sweat shirt, pants torn off at the knees, and a day's growth of beard. He had no pencils, only a battered copy of Harold Robbins' *The Carpetbaggers.* Neither stooge spoke to the real applicants as they worked on self-ratings.

We then compared the evaluations before and after the arrival of the stooge. Mr. Clean produced a sharp drop in self-esteem. Applicants suddenly felt sloppy, stupid and inferior by comparison; indeed, Mr.

Clean was an intimidating character. But Mr. Dirty gave everyone a psychological lift. After his arrival, applicants felt more handsome, confident and optimistic.

We might conclude that the slobs of the world do a great favor for those around them: they raise self-esteem.

SIGNALS. The behavior and appearance of others inspire self-change, but the setting in which we encounter others also exerts an influence. For example, work situations consistently reward serious, steadfast, Calvinistic behavior. But for a person to act this way in all situations would be unfortunate, especially when the situation demands spontaneity and play. No one wants to live with the Protestant Ethic 24 hours a day; in this sense, THE OFFICE DOOR AND THE DOOR TO ONE'S HOME SERVE AS SIGNALS FOR SELF-TRANSFORMATION.

LESSON. Freudian theory awakened us to the motives that underlie behavior; for instance, we have become aware of the self-gratifying aspects of even the most altruistic behavior. I think that we can apply this lesson to the study of public identity. If someone appears open, warm and accepting, we may ask why that person adopts such a mask. We may inquire what the cold and aloof individual hopes to attain with that appearance. We should not, however, conclude that the mask is a sure sign of the person's deep-seated character. When motives change, conviviality may turn to coolness, the open man may become guarded.

We studied the relationship between masks and motives in several experiments, most of them based on approval-seeking. Carl Rogers pointed out that the warm regard of others is vital to feelings of self-regard and hence to feelings of personal worth. So we asked: *How do individuals present themselves when they want to gain the approval of others?*

The warm regard of others is vital to feelings of self-regard and hence to feelings of personal worth.

In experiments designed to answer this question, we varied the characteristics of the other in systematic ways. He might be senior to our subject in authority, or junior; open and reveal-ing, or closed and remote; a stern task-master or an easygoing boss. When an individual seeks approval from this diverse range of personalities, he adopts wholly different masks or public identities. When he is not seeking approval, self-presentation is much different in character.

GLOW. I will use one of our experiments on authority figures as an illustration. A woman who was senior in age and status interviewed 18 under-graduate women. Before the session

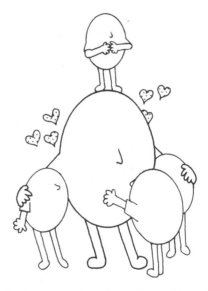

began, we took each student aside and asked if she would help us by trying as best as she could to gain the liking of the interviewer. We told her that she could do or say anything she wished to achieve this goal.

We observed the students' behavior in the interviews; all identified themselves to the interviewer in glowing terms. They indicated they were highly accepting of others, socially popular, perceptive, and industrious in work. Students in the control condition, who had not been instructed to seek approval, showed no such change of masks.

So far, no surprise. What startled us was that this conscious role-playing had marked effects on the students' feelings about themselves. After the interview each student made a private self-appraisal, and we compared her rating to tests she had taken a month earlier. Apparently, in trying to convince the interviewer of their sterling assets, the students succeeded in convincing themselves. There was no such change in self-esteem in the control group.

In subsequent research we found that persons can improve their feelings about themselves simply by thinking about their positive qualities. It is not necessary to act the role; fantasizing about how they would act is sufficient.

PLASTIC. Taken together, our experiments document the remarkable flexibility of the self. We are made of soft plastic, and molded by social circumstances. But we should not conclude that all of our relationships are fake: subjects in our studies generally believed in the masks they wore. Once donned, mask becomes reality.

I do not want to imply that there are no central tendencies in one's concept of self. There are some lessons that we learn over and over, that remain consistent through life—sextyping, for example. Men learn to view themselves as "masculine," women as "feminine." Some of us have been so rigorously trained to see ourselves as "inferior" or "superior" that we become trapped in these definitions. Often we cannot escape even when the self-concepts become inappropriate or unwanted.

But we have paid too much attention to central tendencies, and have ignored the range and complexity of being. The individual has many potential selves. He carries with him the capacity to define himself, as warm or cold, dominant or submissive, sexy or

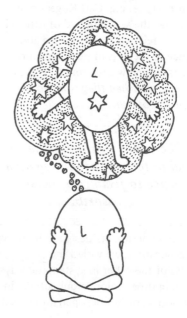

plain. The social conditions around him help determine which of these options are evoked.

We must abandon the assumption that normal development equips the individual with a coherent sense of identity. The individual has many potential selves, and carries with him the capacity to define himself.

I believe we must abandon the assumption that normal development equips the individual with a coherent sense of identity. In the richness of human relations, a person receives varied messages about who he is. Parents, friends, lovers, teachers, kin, counselors, acquaintances all behave differently toward us; in each relationship we learn something new about ourselves and, as the relations change, so do the messages. The lessons are seldom connected and they are often inconsistent.

WORRY. In this light, the value that society places on a coherent identity is unwarranted and possibly detrimental. It means that the heterosexual must worry over homosexual leanings, the husband or wife over fantasies of infidelity, the businessman over his drunken sprees, the commune dweller over his materialism. All of us are burdened by the code of coherence,

which demands that we ask: HOW CAN I BE X, IF I AM REALLY Y, ITS OPPOSITE? We should ask instead: WHAT IS CAUSING ME TO BE X AT THIS TIME? We may be justifiably concerned with tendencies that disrupt our preferred modes of living and loving; but we should not be anxious, depressed or disgusted when we find a multitude of interests, potentials and selves.

Indeed, perhaps our true concern should be aroused when we become too comfortable with ourselves, too fixed in a specific identity. It may mean that our environment has become redundant—we are relating to the same others, we encounter the same situations over and over. Identity may become coherent in this fashion, but it may also become rigid and maladaptive. If a man can see himself only as powerful, he will feel pain when he recognizes moments of weakness. If a woman thinks of herself as active and lively, moments of quiet will be unbearable; if we define ourselves as weak and compliant we will cringe ineptly when we are challenged to lead.

The social structure encourages such one-dimensionality. We face career alternatives, and each decision constricts the possibilities. Our social relationships stabilize as do our professional commitments; eventually we find ourselves in routines that vary little from day to day.

INTIMACY. Many of us seek refuge

from the confining borders and pressures of careers in long-term intimate relationships. Here, we feel, we can be liberated: we can reveal our true selves, give and take spontaneously, be fully honest.

Unfortunately, salvation through intimacy usually is a false hope, based on Western romantic myth. Marriage, we are taught, soothes the soul, cures loneliness, and frees the spirit. It is true that at the outset, love and intimacy provide an experience in personal growth. The loved one comes to see himself as passionate, poetic, vital, attractive, profound, intelligent, and utterly lovable. In the eyes of his beloved, the individual becomes all that he would like to be: he tries on new masks, acts out old fantasies. With the security of love, identity may flower anew.

RIGIDITY. I have had a broad range of experience with young married couples, and I observe that for most of them the myth of marriage dies quickly. In a matter of months they feel the pain of identity constriction; the role of mate becomes stabilized and rigid. I think that such stabilization occurs for at least three reasons:

1. *The reliance of each spouse on the other for fulfillment of essential needs.* To the extent that each partner needs the other for financial support, food preparation, care of children, housekeeping, and so on, stable patterns of behavior must develop. Each begins to hold the other responsible

for certain things, and if these expectations are not met the violator is punished. *But you can't just quit your job,* one asserts; *You call this dinner?* the other complains; and *How many times do I have to tell you not to make plans on Sunday when I'm watching the game?* Interdependency fosters standardized behavior. And along with standardized behavior comes a limited identity.

2. *Our general inability to tolerate inconsistencies in others.* From infancy we learn that, to survive, we must locate the inconsistencies in our environment and maintain them. If we could not predict from moment to moment whether a friend would respond to us with laughter, sadness, boredom or rejection, we would rapidly become incapable of action. Thus we reward consistent identity in others and punish variations. This process eases interaction, makes it predictable, and greases the wheels of social discourse. In an intimate relationship, it also constitutes identity.

3. *Our inability to tolerate extreme emotional states for long periods of time.* The new identities that emerge in the early stage of a relationship depend in part on the emotional intensity of this period—an intensity fired by the discovery of another's love, the risk of trying new masks, the prospect of a major commitment, and sexual arousal. But it is seldom that we can sustain such grand passion, or tolerate the anger and depression that are its inevitable

counterparts. We weary of the emotional roller coaster, and replace passion with peace. It is difficult to restore intense feelings once we have quelled them, though some events may ignite them again temporarily. . . .

AROUND. This picture is depressing, I realize. Probably most of us have friends who now settle for contentment in place of joy, and we know others who ceaselessly search for ecstasy in new relationships—only to see it vanish at the moment of capture. Solutions are elusive, because the tightening of identity moves so slowly that only cumulative effects are visible.

BUT IF WE ARE AWARE OF THE PROCESS THAT LIMITS IDENTITY, WE CAN SUBVERT IT. We can broaden our experiences with others: the more unlike us they are, the more likely we are to be shaken from a rigid sense of identity. Lovers can pursue new experiences:

confront a foreign culture, meet at odd times or places, drastically alter the schedule of who-does-what-and-when, develop individual interests. If each partner presents new demands, the stage is set for trying on new masks—and this in turn awakens new feelings about the self. Honest communication—*this is how I think you are*—is essential. Once in the open, such images usually prove quite false; and as impressions are broken, expectations become more pliable and demands for consistency lose urgency. Finally, if playing a role does in fact lead to real changes in one's self-concept, we should learn to play more roles, to adopt any role that seems enjoyable—a baron, a princess, a secret agent, an Italian merchant—and, if the other is willing to play, a storehouse of novel self-images emerges.

The mask may not be the symbol of superficiality that we have thought it was, but the means of realizing our potential. Walt Whitman wrote:

We can broaden our experiences with others: the more unlike us they are, the more likely we are to be shaken from a rigid sense of identity.

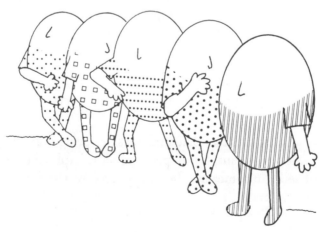

Do I contradict myself?
Very well then, I contradict myself.
(I am large. I contain multitudes.)

❧

HOW DO YOU RESPOND TO GERGEN'S APPROACH?

The earlier article on Marilyn Monroe's life seems to change when I apply Gergen's idea of role-playing to it. Try it, and see what happens in your head.

British psychiatrist R. D. Laing wrote this short brain-twister about "double-bind" role-playing, which shows how complex masks may become:

> *They are playing a game.*
> *They are playing at not playing*
> *a game. If I show them I see*
> *they are, I shall break the rules*
> *and they will punish me. I must*
> *play their game, of not seeing*
> *I see the game.*

EVER BEEN IN THAT KIND OF SITUATION?

Laing suggests that such mask-relating may lead to serious mental health problems, but depending on role-playing for your definition of self can sometimes be funny, too. As the following short story demonstrates. . . .

UP THE WALL

Husband
in Charge

BY ERMA BOMBECK

*"Don't worry about a thing," he said,
when I had to leave for a few days.*

I once read a poll of what husbands think wives do all day long.

The results were rather what you would expect.

Thirty-three percent said women spent five hours out of each day putting lint on their husbands' socks.

Twenty-seven percent said they spent four hours daily pouring grease down the sink and watching it harden to give husbands something to do when they got home.

Ten percent swore their wives held the door open all day to make sure all the warm/cool air (depending on the season) got out of the house.

A walloping 58 percent said women divided their time hiding from the children, watching soap operas, drinking coffee, shrinking shirt collars, discarding one sock from every pair in the drawer, lugging power tools out to the sandbox for the kids to play with and trying to get the chenille creases out of their faces before their husbands came home.

That's the kind of logic you can expect from full-grown men who think that appliances are inanimate and have no feelings of hostility.

I thought a lot about that poll, but I never mentioned it. I figured someday . . . sometime . . . somehow . . . some man would pay for those remarks.

Some man just did.

About three weeks ago, I was summoned to Ohio to help my mother, who had had minor surgery and was going to be flat on her back for a few weeks.

"Are you sure you can handle things around here?" I asked my husband. "The kids, the cooking, the laundry, the routine?"

"Does Dean Martin know how to make a drink?" he asked flatly. "Of course I can handle this stuff. Don't worry about it. You just go off and do what you have to do and don't give us a thought."

I didn't give them a thought until I was paged at the airport just before my flight took off.

"One quick question," said my husband. "What does 'Bwee, no nah, noo' mean?"

"Who said it?"

"Whadaya mean who said it? Your baby just said it and looked kinda desperate."

"It means, 'I have to go to the bathroom.' "

"Oh, well, that's all I needed to know. Have a good . . ."

"It also means, 'I want a cookie. Where are my coloring books? The dog just crawled in the dryer. There's a policeman at the door. I am floating my $20 orthopedic shoes in the john.' The kid has a limited vocabulary and has to double up."

"I can handle this. It's just that she looks so miserable."

"It also means, 'It's too late for the bathroom,' " I said and ran to catch my plane.

There was a message awaiting me at Mother's and I called home before I unpacked.

"What's up?"

"No problem," he said cheerfully. "It's just that Maxine Milshire just called and can't drive the car pool tomorrow because she's subbing for Janice Winerod on the bowling team. She can pick up . . . unless it rains. Her convertible top won't go up. However, if the weather is decent she can pick up and trade with Jo Caldwell who is pregnant and three weeks overdue, but who has a doctor who was weak in math. That means I will drive Thursday unless Jo Caldwell's doctor lucks out. In that case I'll have an early meeting and it might rain. Do you understand any of this?"

"No."

"I'll call you tomorrow night."

The next night I answered the phone. There was a brief silence.

"Well, I hope you're happy, Missy. I am now the only 38-year-old boy in my office who has been exposed to roseola. I was late for work because little Buster Smarts was eating chili off the dashboard of my car and spilled it all over the upholstery; and my job is in jeopardy."

"Why is your job in jeopardy?" I asked.

"Because YOUR son answered the phone this morning while I was putting catchup on sandwiches and I heard him tell Mr. Weems, 'Daddy can't come to the phone now. He's hitting the bottle.' "

"Tomorrow is Saturday. It'll get better," I promised.

The phone rang early Saturday.

"Hello," I giggled, "this is Dial-a-Prayer."

"Oh, you're cute," he snarled, "real cute. Just a couple of questions here. First, where are the wheels off the sweeper?"

"On the back of the bicycle in the garage."

"Check. Where does the washer walk to when it walks?"

"It never gets any farther than the door."

"Check. When was the last time you were in the boys' bedroom?"

"1969."

"Check. What do you do when you have perma-scorched all the perma-press?"

"I'll be home in two days," I said.

When he didn't call me on Sunday, I called him.

"I can't talk now," he said irritably.

"Why not? What's the matter?"

"Nothing is the matter. I bought a box of chicken for dinner and the box caught fire in the oven."

"You're supposed to . . ."

"Don't say it or I'll hang up. Then YOUR baby chose a rather inopportune time to get a penny stuck up her nose; I've got 35 boys in the bathroom watching movies; I just tried to make a drink and there are no ice cubes; and I've been named Homeroom Mother."

I arrived home early in the morning before the family was up. My husband staggered to the door. "My wife gives at the office," he mumbled.

"I'm home," I announced. "Tell me, why is there an X chalked on the side of our house?"

He rubbed his eyes tiredly.

"A baby-sitter put it there. I think we're marked for demolition."

I wandered through the house thinking it was too late. The dog was drinking out of the ashtray. There was a pad of blank checks by the phone with messages scribbled on them. The blackboard had a single message on it:

"I am leaving and I am not coming back. Daddy."

"Why is the baby sleeping in the bathtub?" I asked.

"She drank four glasses of water just before bedtime."

"There is a crease on your face shaped like a duck."

"I had to separate the boys so I slept in the baby's bed."

36   I opened up the refrigerator. A leftover reached for me and I slammed the door shut.

After breakfast, my husband smiled and leaned over to kiss the boys good-bye. They turned away. "He murdered our guppies," one of them snapped.

"We'll talk about that tonight," he said.

Then he turned toward me. "Good-bye, dear. You'll find everything shipshape. I mean, all you have to have is a routine. By the way," he whispered, "could you call and let me know how Lisa makes out in *As the World Turns*?"

As I watched him swing toward the garage, I thought to myself that he looked too old to be carrying a Donald Duck thermos, a security blanket, and sporting a red rash on his neck.

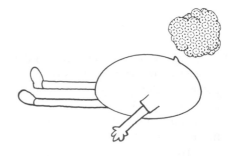

So far we've seen two approaches to defining self.

      (1) self-concept
      (2) multiple role-playing

BUT WE AIN'T THROUGH, FOLKS!

Yet *another* avenue is taken by Dr. Seymour Fisher in the following
article. In some ways both of the approaches we've looked at blend into
what Dr. Fisher has to say.

See if you can spot the connections, as he raps on. . . .

Experiencing Your Body:
You Are
What You Feel

There is no more fascinating sight than your own image looking back at you in a mirror. You are drawn to it in a half-embarrassed way, excited and intensely involved. Do you remember the last time someone showed you a photograph of yourself? Wasn't there a surge of feeling and a deep curiosity about "How do I look?" Perhaps, too, you have noticed the strange entrancement even animals display at the sight of their mirror double.

Your body encompasses a sector of space that is uniquely your own. It represents your base of operations in the world, the outward manifestation of your being and identity. No other object is so persistently with you. Unceasingly, even when you are asleep, you receive enormous quantities of information from your body. Your decisions, fantasies, even your dreams are influenced by the sensations emanating from it. Yet it is only in the last two decades that serious scientific attention has been given to the study of the body as a *psychological* phenomenon.

For centuries scientists have studied the body as an anatomical structure and a biological system, leaving its psychological aspects to other disciplines. Artists and writers, for example, traditionally have devoted great energy to capturing the "feel" of the body in dramatic contexts. Eastern philosophies such as yoga have enjoyed a considerable measure of Western popularity in recent years, in part because of their supposed power to put the individual closer to his own body. Similarly, the so-called "drug culture" has drawn on

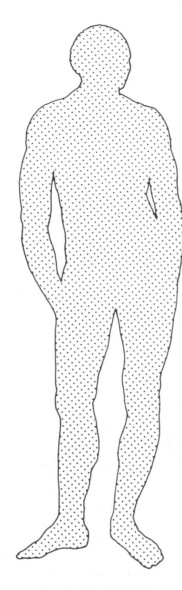

38

body experience; LSD users, for example, report that the chemical frequently produces the feeling that parts of the body have become detached or that the boundary between the body and the outside world has disappeared.

But even the average person must admit to a curiosity about his body and a preoccupation with the psychological experiences it presents to him. He is concerned about the impression his body makes on others; he experiences anxiety about the potential vulnerability of his body to disease and trauma; he uses "gut" cues to help him decide whether or not to get involved with certain people or confront certain situations; he puts out large sums of money to shape and camouflage his appearance so that it will conform to his idealized concept of the "good body." Indeed, a major portion of advertising is devoted to products that claim to improve the individual's relationship with his body—by making it cleaner, more fragrant, stronger, sexier.

The task of making sense of our own bodies is not as simple as we might hope or expect. As each individual matures, he is confronted with the problems of *integrating* an endless barrage of sensations and assimilating the meaning adults ascribe to various sectors of his frame. HE DISCOVERS COMPLICATED RULES PRESCRIBING THE AREAS HE CAN TOUCH, TALK ABOUT, LOOK AT, AND EVEN THINK ABOUT. He is puzzled by the multiple, and often opposed meanings assigned to the same body area. He learns, for example, that the back of his body is simultaneously a spatial dimension, a place where punishment is applied, and a locus for concern about anal sphincter control; yet the same area also remains obscure because he cannot even get a direct view of it.

The child's attempt to construct a complete psychological map of his body is further hindered by the negative messages he receives from others about such an enterprise. His parents are reluctant to talk about body events, and, in fact, become angry or embarrassed when he explicitly mentions certain organs or orifices. He learns that the available vocabulary for describing his own body experiences is

sparse and tinged with an illicit flavor. Moreover, the child soon realizes that the culture does not trust body experiences; his education focuses on cultivating intellectual capacities, but his teachers insist that he control body impulses that are likely to "break out" if not closely monitored.

The child soon learns that the culture does not trust body experiences.

Growing up in such an atmosphere, a child finds it almost impossible to examine or codify his body experiences realistically. Hasty glimpses of body terrain and fragments of anatomical information must be pieced together with little or no outside help. For these reasons, the individual is inclined to view his body as

40 having alien qualities and to entertain numerous irrational notions about it.

In fact, although an individual experiences his body more often and in far greater depth than he does any other object in his environment, his perceptions of this, his dearest possession, remain distorted throughout his life. For example, when the average person is called upon to describe or make judgments about his body, he displays considerable inaccuracy. In studies in which persons have been asked to indicate the sizes of various body parts (e.g., head, arms), they often grossly over or underestimate their true proportions.

How well do we know our bodies?

discover on meeting an old friend after a long separation that the friend perceives much greater signs of aging than the individual had recognized in himself.

This lag is especially apparent in the blind. For example, a man of middle age who had lost his sight when he was young told me that his image of himself was still that of the child he had last seen in the mirror years ago. Although others responded to him as a middle-aged adult, he could only visualize himself physically in the form of a young boy.

The so-called "phantom limb" provides another striking example of

PEOPLE DIFFER IN HOW CLEARLY THEY PERCEIVE THEIR BODY TO HAVE A DEFENSIVE SHEATH CAPABLE OF PROTECTING THEM.

One of the problems of maintaining an accurate picture of your own body is that the image needs to be repeatedly revised. There is often a lag between the occurrence of change in your body and the incorporation of this change into your body model.

Consider the effects of aging. Many people have been startled to

the difficulty in keeping one's body image up to date. When a person loses a projecting part such as an arm or a nose because of trauma or surgery, he often continues to experience that part as if it were still present. After a while, however, the phantom limb fades and usually disappears permanently.

Although it is difficult for an individual to use body cues rationally, there is no doubt that whatever model he *does* evolve strongly influences his behavior. A person who regards his body as weak and fragile will behave less boldly than one who perceives his body as a well-defended place. Similarly, a person who turns away from his body because he experiences it as bad and ugly may turn to intellectual activities as compensation.

An individual's feelings of boundary security are correlated with how clearly he is aware of his boundary sheath—skin and muscle. Heightened awareness of this sheath seems to contribute to a sense of being adequately bounded and thus more secure.

Many of us have employed this trick in fearful surroundings. Lying in bed, a home owner becomes anxious about a break-in and pictures the enclosing walls of his house. A driver entering a storm assures himself of his safety by glancing at the walls of his metal cocoon. Perhaps even more common is the preference many people have for small bedrooms or tight-fitting clothing.

A person's body experience may permeate his outlook in a number of unique ways. Studies have shown that if a subject is asked to compose imaginative stories, his tales will be affected by whether he is lying down or sitting up; his judgment of how far away an object is will depend on whether or not he feels the object has a meaningful relationship to his body;

his beliefs about how friendly others are toward him may depend upon his faith in the security of his body boundaries, and so forth.

How well we know our body.

It would be impossible for anyone to attend simultaneously to all of the things happening in his body. He would be overwhelmed and ultimately confused. Just as one learns to attend to only certain auditory stimuli, each person must learn to attend to the various sectors of his body in some pattern that is meaningful and useful to him. Each individual . . . actually is rather consistent in his style of distributing body attention, although such consistency holds true more for men than women. One man may be unusually aware of his head, another of his legs, and still another of the right as compared with the left side of his body. What is an outstanding body landmark for one may be almost invisible for another. Also, we have learned that each body sector is associated with a fairly distinct conflict or tension theme.

Most likely, the individual's investment of attention in specific body areas has some adaptive or control function. This is somewhat analogous to a piece of string that is tied around a child's finger when he is sent to the store so that he will remember what he is supposed to buy when he gets there. An individual's long-term focus of attention on a body area could serve, therefore, as a kind of "string around the finger" reminding him that certain things

42 should or should not be done.

In view of the obvious differences between male and female bodies, it would be logical to expect that men and women would construct quite different images of their bodies. We do, in fact, find radically different styles of body perception related to sex.

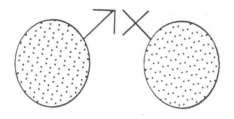

It has been demonstrated that the average woman perceives her body to be better protected and enclosed by a more secure boundary than does the average man. In one study we found that the male was more disturbed by the threat of injecting adrenaline into his body than was the female. Several appraisals of males and females hospitalized for surgery reveal greater anxiety in men than in women about the body-threatening implications of the situation. Men may carefully control their open expression of such anxiety, but inwardly they are more disturbed than women.

In addition to the perception of body threat, there is another important difference in the way males and females experience their bodies. Diverse sources have noted that WOMEN ARE MORE AWARE OF THEIR BODY FEELINGS THAN ARE MEN AND THAT THEY ARE MORE POSITIVE IN ACCEPTING THESE EXPERIENCES. David J. Van Lennep reported that female children not only display their greater body awareness than male children, but the magnitude of this difference between the sexes becomes larger after adolescence. In addition, the degree of body awareness in women is known to be correlated with positive attributes such as a CLEAR SENSE OF IDENTITY, while in men it is linked with certain categories of conflictual preoccupation. This confirms what we already observe in everyday life. Girls and women invest much more open interest in the body than do their male counterparts. They feel free to study their own appearance and to experiment with techniques for altering it by means of clothing and cosmetics. A male who displays much direct or open interest in his body (except with reference to athletic activities) is regarded as a deviant.

A woman sees a clearer relationship between her body and her life role than does a man.

A woman apparently sees a clearer relationship between her body and her life role than a man. Despite the influence of Women's Liberation, the chief goals of most women still revolve about being attractive, entering into marriage, and producing children. Such aims readily permit the female to

see her body as a vehicle for her life
career. This is not true for the man.
Unless he becomes a professional
athlete, he can perceive little connection between his body attributes and
the requirements for status and
success. Male power and accomplish-
ment are increasingly defined in terms
of intellect, cleverness, business
acumen, and so forth. The low status
jobs are the ones that require body
strength.

It is interesting that heightened
concern with body experience has
coincided with the investigation of
body image in the psychological
laboratories and clinics. Indeed, there
is little doubt that the body image is
one of the most important—and,
ironically, most neglected—phenomena
in the scientific quest for understanding of our psychological selves.

43

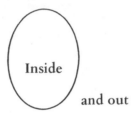

Inside and out

*impossible
locations—*

*reaching in
from out*

*side, out
from in-*

*side—as
middle:*

*one
hand*

ROBERT CREELEY
Pieces

44   Well, that makes three ways I can define my self. They are interrelated and overlapping, yet each has its own central thrust.

I can define my self mentally.

I can define my self socially.

I can define my self physically.

Or I can choose a combination of these perspectives.

The one thing all three approaches have in common is that they assume "self" is something found or realized *within* my skin. True, this self may be developed through dialogue with the environment, but its existence is internal once it is structured/ formed. In each example we've seen, my consciousness, my "I," ends at the skin line. My identity is prisoner in a jail of epidermis; body hair, pores, and freckles are the limits of my being. Alan Watts calls this the "bag of skin" view of identity.

One result of accepting this approach to self-definition is that you and I are forever separate and apart. Communication can occur only through symbols that pass between us; we will never share true awareness of one another because you cannot experience me and vice versa. My "I" and your "I" are sealed off from one another by skin walls.

This bag of skin assumption about self is open to serious challenge, I think. Even a walk in my garden raises questions in my mind. For example, the carrots in my garden spread their beautifully lacy leaves above ground and produce oxygen that is available to me to breathe. At *what point,* if any, does that oxygen stop being a part of a carrot's identity? When does that oxygen become part of my identity? When I inhale that oxygen, do I get a deed of possession that means my self has expanded to include this gas? And when I breathe out carbon dioxide, and a carrot breathes it in (they do, you know), have I lost some of my "I" to that carrot?

Let's play with this just a little longer. When I planted my garden, I made sure the soil contained a great amount of compost (decomposed organic material). That compost included grass clippings, shredded leaves, cow manure, ground limestone, hay, and vegetable pulp from our juice maker. The regular water used to irrigate the garden contains many minerals from stream beds, etc., all of which were gratefully accepted by my thirsty carrot. Question: How can my carrot have an

"identity" apart from the elements it has drawn from the garden—some of which I supplied. Does this mean that part of my "I" is no longer, but is now part of the carrot's "I"?

Question: If I pull up a carrot and eat it, does it lose its identity just because it now changes to human tissue, human feces, and carbon dioxide? Is there any real stopping point in this cycle of all living things? Is it sane to speak of separateness when living seems a process of mutuality?

In spite of the obvious yin-yang qualities, the arising mutually of all life forms, the ecology of this world clearly demonstrating the *interdependence* of all livingness and all nonlivingness—OM spite of all this evidence—the acceptance of separateness of identity is popular in Western psychology and social psychology today. The bag of skin self rules our thinking.

Perhaps more delightful and fully as productive an approach to identity is possible: *I can define my self as all human being.* This is a

46   fourth option to definition. That is, my "I" is the same as your "I"; the apparent difference is the illusion of culture viewpoint. We *are* the same creature, expressing our self in different forms. We are BEING . . . human. As "individuals" you and I are different flames of the same fire, ripples of the same stream, seeds of the same fruit.

    This perspective is, of course, Hindu.

    The illusion of living only in a physical world, and of being a separate entity, is called by the Hindu *maya*. Without this illusion, so it is taught, we might realize that we are different from one another BECAUSE we need contrast and comparison to provoke us to play the cosmic game of discovering our one body. The illusion of the bag of skin identity is necessary for us to "re-member" (pull back together *our* self). Illusion is always essential in the game of hide-and-seek. We must appear separate even to play. But our interdependence demonstrates that we have something in common; we really cannot do without one another. And to understand this is the essential key to going beyond *maya*.

    Jesus expressed this perception of self-as-all when he said: "I am in my Father, and ye in me, and I in you." And in one way or another this same experience is pointed to by other realized beings. Lao-tse in the Tao, Gotama Buddha's Nirvana, Mohammed's Allah, and Moses' Jehovah.

> *yes, yes,*
>   *that's what*
> *I wanted,*
>   *I always wanted,*
> *I always wanted,*
>   *to return*
> *to the body*
>   *where I was born*

ALLEN GINSBERG

Of course, the men I just mentioned were/are *not* modern psychologists. These men were/are without Ph.D.'s, without academic or professional status, and without property. Their statements admittedly do not fit in the behaviorist's laboratory, the theorist's numerous journals, or the psychotherapist's office. It is even unlikely that such an idea of "identity" will be found in general psychology classrooms.

It just isn't popular.

But I feel it *is* appropriate here, since you and I are looking for real possibilities—not formulas. Poet and folk singer Ric Masten has experienced something of this last possibility, if his poem "Demian's Mirror" reflects accurately:

At a corner table
alone and afraid
holding a book
upsidedown
like a bird
come from nowhere
in a dead tree
i'm sitting there
looking around
then i spied a stranger
gazing at me
through glasses
with gold
at the rim
i saw my reflection
looking at me
as i sat there
looking at him

look
in the mirror
demian's mirror

come see yourself
in my glass

the face
it was ageless
a boy in his teens
an old man
a hundred and three
the face of a woman
or was it a man
whose eyes
were fastened on me
i beckoned
the stranger
come over to me
somehow
i felt we had met
i asked
do i know you
he smiled to himself
and said

48

my
how quick they forget

look
in the mirror
demian's mirror
come see yourself
in my glass

we studied
each other
in that dim cafe
and i tried to guess
at his race
what does it matter
he said with a shrug
his spectacles
flashed in his face
i asked
his religion
christian
he said
but i am an atheist too
and sometimes
a buddhist
sometimes a jew

but right now
i'm looking at you

look
in the mirror
demian's mirror
come see yourself
in my glass

he told me his story
talked of his life
his words
made me laugh
made me cry
it was so funny
it was so sad
his life
was exactly like mine
we sat there together
till i fell asleep
and when i woke
he was gone
and all of the mirrors
were smiling at me
and out in the street
it was dawn

All right.
Having read through four possible ways of defining your self, has anything stuck to your face?

WHICH APPROACH FEELS RIGHT TO YOU?

WHO ARE YOU . . . RIGHT NOW?

Only when "I" know WHO I AM
Will "I" know what is possible

BABA RAM DASS
Be Here Now: Remember

3

Being
in
Relationship

Whatever "self" you have grown in the garden of your life, you probably spend much of your day tending, enriching, and protecting it from harmful pests. Every good gardener does, because he wants the healthiest harvest possible.

"Tending the garden of the self" is one way of thinking about human be-ing. And a large part of such soul tilling occurs as we relate to others. Any gardener depends upon the goodwill and cooperation of other creatures.

pp. 51-59 for weds.

51

SIT STILL IN YOUR GARDEN AND LISTEN; SEE WHAT I SAY. Birds, insects, worms, and microorganisms busily churn their energies with sun, soil, and water to raise nourishing crops.

In the same way, only balanced human relationships will sustain nourishing personal growth. Everything is process and relationship, and if our communication is to encourage growth *we must live a healthy interpersonal ecology.* Good friends and loving hands do not thrive in barren soil.

HOW DOES YOUR GARDEN GROW?

IS YOUR RELATIONSHIP "SOIL" FERTILE?

DO YOU KNOW HOW TO GARDEN WELL?

Perhaps the creatures of the garden are fortunate in not having to adjust to human culture, as we do. It may be easier to stay close to basic truths of life if we are not confronted with our socially complex and arbitrary rules of performance, most of which have nothing to do with nature's reality.

My backyard garden has given me some of my most important

guidelines for cultivating nourishing human contact. There I see that truly significant forces are simple and direct. Little is wasted. Nothing is unessential. In my garden the only bullshit I find is on the ground, working as an organic complement to the soil and plants and insects.

How unlike much of my daily "street life."

And in my associations with my fellow humans I miss the realness and directness I find in my backyard universe. But applying my garden lessons to my relationships is *so* hard sometimes.

It occurs to me that I usually listen more fully to my carrots than I do to people.

I mean . . . REALLY listen.

DO YOU KNOW WHAT I MEAN?

Let me share with you a short story that deals with the cultivating skill of listening. It was written by a man who understands the soil of human relationships, John Berry. His tale is entitled:

THE LISTENER

Once there was a puny Czech concert violinist named Rudolf, who lived in Sweden. Some of his friends thought he was not the best of musicians because he was restless; others thought he was restless because he was not the best of musicians.

At any rate, he hit upon a way of making a living, with no competitors. Whether by choice or necessity, he used to sail about Scandinavia in his small boat, all alone, giving concerts in little seaport towns. If he found an accompanist, well and good; if not, he played works for unaccompanied violin; and it happened once or twice that he wanted a piano so badly that he imagined one, and then he played whole sonatas for violin and piano, with no piano in sight.

One year Rudolf sailed all the way out to Iceland and began working his way around that rocky coast from one town to another. It was a hard, stubborn land; but people in those difficult places do not forget the law of hospitality to the stranger—for their God may decree that they too shall become strangers on the face of the earth. The audiences were small, and even if Rudolf had been really first-rate, they would not have been very demonstrative. From ancient times their energy had gone, first of all, into earnest toil. Sometimes they were collected by the local school teacher, who reminded

them of their duty to the names of Beethoven and Bach and Mozart and one or two others whose music perhaps was not much heard in those parts. Too often people sat stolidly watching the noisy little fiddler, and went home feeling gravely edified. But they paid.

As Rudolf was sailing from one town to the next along a sparsely settled shore, the northeast turned black and menacing. A storm was bearing down upon Iceland. Rudolf was rounding a bleak, dangerous cape, and his map told him that the nearest harbor was half a day's journey away. He was starting to worry when he saw, less than a mile off shore, a lighthouse on a tiny rock island. With some difficulty, in the rising seas, he put in there and moored to an iron ring that hung from the cliff. A flight of stairs, hewn out of the rock, led up to the lighthouse. On top of the cliff, outlined against the scudding clouds, stood a man.

"You are welcome!" the voice boomed over the sound of the waves that were already beginning to break over the island.

Darkness fell quickly. The lighthouse keeper led his guest up the spiral stairs to the living room on the third floor, then busied himself in preparation for the storm. Above all, he had to attend to the great lamp in the tower, that dominated the whole region. It was a continuous light, intensified by reflectors, and eclipsed by shutters at regular intervals. The duration of the light was equal to that of darkness.

The lighthouse keeper was a huge old man with a grizzled beard that came down over his chest. Slow, deliberate, bearlike, he moved without wasted motion about the limited world of which he was the master. He spoke little, as if words had not much importance compared to the other forces that comprised his life. Yet he was equable, as those elements were not.

After the supper of black bread and boiled potatoes, herring, cheese and hot tea, which they took in the kitchen above the living room, the two men sat and contemplated each other's presence. Above them was the maintenance room, and above that the great lamp spoke majestic, silent messages of light to the ships at sea. The storm hammered like a battering ram on the walls of the lighthouse. Rudolf offered tobacco, feeling suddenly immature as he did so. The old man smiled a little as he declined it by a slight movement of his head; it was as if he knew well the uses of tobacco and the need for offering it, and affirmed it all, yet—here he, too, was halfway apologetic—was self-contained and without need of anything that was not already within his power. And he sat there, gentle and reflective, his great workman hands resting on outspread thighs.

It seemed to Rudolf that the lighthouse keeper was entirely aware of all the sounds of the storm and of its violent impact upon the lighthouse, but he knew them so well that he did not have to think about them; they were like the voluntary movements of his own heart and blood. In the same way, beneath the simple courtesy that made him speak and listen to his guest in specific ways, he was already calmly and mysteriously a part of him, as surely as the mainland was connected with the little island, and all the islands with one another, so commodiously, under the ocean.

Gradually Rudolf drew forth the sparse data of the old man's life: He had been born in this very lighthouse eighty-three years before, when his father was the lighthouse keeper. His mother—the only woman he had ever known—taught him to read the Bible, and he read it daily. He had no other books.

As a musician, Rudolf had not had time to read much either—but then, he lived in cities. He reached down and took his beloved violin out of its case.

"What do you make with that, sir?" the old man asked.

For a second Rudolf thought his host might be joking; but serenity of the other's expression reassured him. There was not even curiosity about the instrument, but rather a whole interest in him, the person, that included his "work." In most circumstances Rudolf would have found it hard to believe that there could exist someone who did not know what a violin was; yet now he had no inclination to laugh. He felt small and inadequate.

"I make—music with it," he stammered in a low tone.

"Music," the old man said ponderously. "I have heard of it. But I have never seen music."

"One does not see music. One hears it."

"Ah, yes," the lighthouse keeper consented, as it were with humility. This too was in the nature of things wherein all works were wonders, and all things were known eternally and were poignant in their transiency. His wide gray eyes rested upon the little fiddler and conferred upon him all the importance of which any individual is capable.

Then something in the storm and the lighthouse and the old man exalted Rudolf, filled him with compassion, and love and a spaciousness infinitely beyond himself. He wanted to strike a work of fire and stars into being for the old man. And, with the storm as

his accompanist, he stood and began to play—the Kreutzer Sonata of Beethoven.

The moments passed, moments that were days in the creation of that world of fire and stars; abysses and heights of passionate struggle, the idea of order, and the resolution of these in the greatness of the human spirit. Never before had Rudolf played with such mastery—or with such an accompanist. Waves and wind beat the tower with giant hands. Steadily above them the beacon raced in its sure cycles of darkness and light. The last note ceased and Rudolf dropped his head on his chest, breathing hard. The ocean seethed over the island with a roar as of many voices.

The old man had sat unmoving through the work, his broad gnarled hands resting on his thighs, his head bowed, listening massively. For some time he continued to sit in silence.

Then he looked up, lifted those hands calmly, judiciously, and nodded his head.

"Yes," he said. "That is true."

WOULD YOU LIKE TO BE LISTENED TO BY THIS OLD MAN?

DO YOU THINK THE NATURE OF HIS "SELF" HAS ANYTHING TO DO WITH THE WAY HE COMMUNICATES?

IS RUDOLF AN EFFECTIVE COMMUNICATOR, IN YOUR OPINION?

When I read this story I felt so awed and moved by the intimacy and fullness given and accepted by the old man that I wept. I admit that this experience of being heard, as Rudolf was so completely, is not common in my life. Coming or going. Giving or taking.

IS IT IN YOURS?

When I think about it, it seems that I have learned *not* to pay close attention to people . . . or things, for that matter. I wonder why it is I

58 so seldom expect others to really hear what's going on inside me? Think there's a connection, don't you? Poet Ric Masten would agree:

i have just
wandered back
into our conversation
and find
that you
are still
rattling on
about something
or other
i think i must
have been gone
at least
twenty minutes

and you
never missed me

now
this might say

something
about my
acting ability
or it might say
something about
your sensitivity

one thing
troubles me tho
when it
is my turn
to rattle on
for twenty minutes
which i
have been known to do

have you
been missing too

A healthy garden cannot exist without the active INVOLVEMENT of its creatures and elements. Clear perception of one another is an issue of survival there. Can you imagine soil not understanding the presence of rain; plants ignoring the reality of sunlight; the tender roots of seedlings not "listening" for available nourishment?

Is this not equally true in interpersonal ecology, be-ing human?

Can we expect to harvest nourishing relationships without active INVOLVEMENT in their growth? I don't believe so. Barren soil produces nothing. Nourishment begets nourishment.

DO YOU HAVE ANY NOURISHING HUMAN RELATIONSHIPS?

DO YOU HAVE ANY BARREN HUMAN RELATIONSHIPS?

DO YOU HAVE ANY TOXIC HUMAN RELATIONSHIPS?

EXACTLY *WHAT* MAKES THE DIFFERENCE BETWEEN THEM?

In the short story that follows, try to pick out the behaviors *you* consider nourishing and those *you* consider toxic. Then evaluate the relationships involved and the quality of the human gardening. I think you'll find the authoress, Carson McCullers, a sensitive farmer.

SUCKER

It was always like I had a room to myself. Sucker slept in a bed near me but he didn't interfere with anything. The room was mine, and I used it like I wanted to.

Whenever I'd bring any of my friends back to my room, all I had to do was just glance once at Sucker, and he'd get up from whatever he was busy with and maybe half-smile at me and leave without saying a word. He never brought kids back there. He's twelve, four years younger than I am, and he always knew without me even telling him that I didn't want kids that age messing with my things.

Most of the time I used to forget that Sucker isn't my brother. He's my cousin but practically ever since I remember he's been in our family. His folks were killed in a wreck when he was a baby. To ma and my kid sisters he was like our brother.

Sucker used to remember and believe every word I told him. That's how he got his nickname. Once a couple of years ago I told him that if he'd jump off our garage with an umbrella, it would act as a parachute and he wouldn't fall hard. He did it and busted his knee. That's just one instance. And the funny thing was that no matter how many times he got fooled he would still believe me. Not that he was dumb in other ways—it was just the way he acted with me.

He used to talk to himself a lot when he'd think he was alone—all about him fighting gangsters and being on ranches and that sort of kid stuff. Usually, though, he was very quiet. He didn't have many boys in the neighborhood to buddy with, and his face had the look of a kid who is watching a game and waiting to be asked to

neg. (handwritten annotation)

positive strokes to himself (handwritten annotation)

60 play. That was Sucker up until a few months ago when all this trouble began.

Maybelle Watts was somehow mixed up in what happened, so I guess I ought to start with her. It is impossible to describe Maybelle. All the boys were crazy about her, but she didn't even notice me. Between classes I used to try and pass very close to her in the halls, but she would hardly ever smile at me. *discount*

That went on for nearly three months and then somehow Maybelle began to change. In the halls she *plastic stroke* would speak to me and every morning she copied my homework. Then one lunchtime I danced with her in the gym and knew everything was going to change.

It was that night when this trouble really started. I had come into my room late, and Sucker was already asleep. I felt happy and keyed up and was awake thinking about Maybelle a long time. The house was quiet and when Sucker spoke, it was a shock to me.

"Pete?"

I didn't answer or even move.

pos. "You do like me as if I was your own brother, don't you, Pete?"

"Sure," I said.

"No matter what you did, I always knew you liked me."

I was wide awake, and my mind seemed mixed up in a strange way. I guess you understand people better when you are happy than when something is worrying you.

pos. "You're a good kid, Sucker," I said.

We talked for a long time that night. His voice was fast, and it was like he had been saving up these things to tell me for a long time. He said he was going to try to build a canoe and *neg.* that the kids down the block wouldn't *o.* let him in on their football team and I don't know what all. I talked some, too, and it was a good feeling to think of him taking in everything I said so seriously. I even spoke of Maybelle a little, only I made out like it was her who had been running after me all this time. He asked questions about high school. His voice was excited, and he kept on talking fast like he could never get the words out in time. When I went to sleep, he was still talking.

During the next couple of weeks I saw a lot of Maybelle. She acted as though she really cared for me a little. Half the time I felt so good that I hardly knew what to do.

pos. But I didn't forget about Sucker. There were a lot of old things in my bureau drawer I'd been saving—boxing gloves and second-rate fishing tackle. All this I turned over to Sucker. We had some more talks, and it was really like I was knowing him for the first time. When there was a long cut on his cheek, I knew he had been monkeying around with this new razor of mine, but I didn't say anything.

I guess things went on like this for about a month or six weeks. I couldn't settle down to study or put my mind on anything. I wanted to be friendly with everybody. There were times when I just had to talk to someone. And usually that would be Sucker. Once he said, "Pete, I am glad you're like a brother." *pos .*

Then something happened between Maybelle and me. I never figured out just what it was. I'd see her out riding with this guy on the football team who had a yellow car the color of her hair. After school she would ride off with him, laughing and looking into his face. *pos .*

I couldn't think of anything to do about it, and she was on my mind all day and night. When I did get a chance to go out with her, she was bored and didn't seem to notice me. *neg .*

At first I was so worried I just forgot about Sucker. Then later he began to get on my nerves. He was always hanging around until I would get home from high school. Then I wouldn't say anything, and he would finally go out.

I can't divide that time up and say this happened one day and that the next. For one thing I was so mixed up that the weeks just slid along into each other. Maybelle still rode around with this guy, and sometimes she would smile at me and sometimes not. Every afternoon I went from one place to another where I thought she'd be.

Sucker kept getting on my nerves more and more. He looked as though he sort of blamed me for something, but at the same time knew that it wouldn't last long.

Then the finish came between Maybelle and me. I met her going to the drugstore and asked her for a date. When she said no, I said something smart. She told me she was sick and *discount* tired of my being around and that she had never really cared about me. I just stood there and didn't answer anything. I walked home slowly.

For several afternoons I stayed in my room by myself. I didn't want to go anywhere or talk to anyone. When Sucker would come in and look at me sort of funny, I'd yell at him to get *neg .* out. I didn't want to think of Maybelle, and I sat at my desk reading or whittling at a toothbrush rack I was trying to make.

Then one night Sucker woke me up again.

"Pete, what's the matter with you?"

All of a sudden I felt mad—at *neg* myself and Maybelle and Sucker and *discounting himself* every single person I knew. I remembered all the times Maybelle had humiliated me and everything bad that ever happened. It was as if nobody would ever like me but a sap like Sucker.

"Why is it we aren't buddies like we were before? Why—"

"*neg* Shut your mouth!" I jumped up and turned on the light. He sat in the middle of his bed, his eyes blinking and scared.

There was something in me, and I couldn't help myself. Words came without me knowing what they would be. It was only afterward that I

62 remembered each thing I said.

"Why aren't we buddies? Because you're the dumbest slob I ever saw! *neg.* Nobody cares anything about you! *neg.* Just because I felt sorry for you sometimes and tried to act decent, don't think I give a hang for a dumb little creep like you!" *discount*

If I'd talked loud or hit him, it wouldn't have been so bad. But my voice was slow, and I was very calm. Sucker's mouth was partway open, and sweat came out on his forehead.

"Don't you know a single thing?" I said. "Haven't you ever been around at all? What kind of a sissy do you want to grow up to be anyway?" *neg.*

I didn't know what was coming next. I couldn't help myself or think.

He didn't move. He had on one of my pajama jackets, and his neck stuck out skinny and small. His hair was damp on his forehead.

"Why do you always hang around me? Don't you know when you're not wanted?" *neg.*

Afterward I could remember the change in Sucker's face. Slowly that blank look went away, and he closed his mouth. His eyes got narrow and his fist shut. I'd never seen such a look on him before. It was like every second he was getting older—getting a hard look to his eyes that seemed wrong in a kid. A drop of sweat rolled down his chin, and he didn't notice. He just sat with those eyes on me and didn't speak, and his face didn't move.

"No, you don't know when you're not wanted. You're too dumb. Just like your name—a dumb Sucker."

It was like something had busted inside me. I turned off the lights and sat down by the window. My legs were shaking, and I was so tired I could have bawled. I sat there a long time. After a while I heard Sucker lie down. I wasn't mad anymore, only tired. It seemed awful to me that I had talked like that to a kid only twelve. I told myself I would try to make it up. I planned how I could straighten it out in the morning. Then trying not to squeak the springs, I got back in bed.

Sucker was gone when I woke up the next day. And later when I went *pos.* to apologize, he looked at me in this *neg.* new hard way so that I couldn't say a word.

All that was two or three months ago. Since then Sucker has grown faster than any boy I ever saw. He's almost as tall as I am, and his bones have gotten heavier and bigger. He won't wear my old clothes any more. *neg.* Our room isn't mine at all now. He's gotten up this gang of kids, and they have a club. When they aren't playing in some vacant lot and fighting, they're always in my room. They've rigged up a radio and every afternoon it blares out music. *neg.*

It's even worse when we are in the room. He sprawls across his bed and *neg.* just stares at me with that hard, half-sneering look. I fiddle around my desk and can't get settled. The thing is I have to study because I've gotten three bad grades this term already. If I flunk English, I can't graduate next year.

I don't care a flip for Maybelle anymore, and it's only this thing between Sucker and me that's the trouble now. We never speak except when we have to in front of the family. I don't even want to call him Sucker anymore, and unless I forget, I call him by his real name, Richard. At night I can't study with him in the room, and I hang around the drugstore with the guys who loaf there.

I've sometimes thought that if we could have it out in a big fight, it would help. But I can't fight him because he's four years younger. And another thing—sometimes this look in his eyes makes me almost believe that *meg.* if Sucker could, he would kill me.

⚜

IN THE FIRST HALF OF THE STORY, WAS THE RELATIONSHIP BETWEEN PETE AND SUCKER TOXIC OR NOURISHING?

WHAT BEHAVIORS CHANGED IN THE SECOND HALF?

HAVE YOU EVER BEEN A "SUCKER" TO ANYONE? HOW DID YOU ACT IN THAT RELATIONSHIP?

COMPARED WITH THE RELATIONSHIP OF THE LIGHTHOUSE KEEPER AND THE VIOLINIST, HOW DO YOU RATE PETE AND SUCKER'S COMMUNICATION?

HOW DO YOU RATE EACH BOY AS A *LISTENER?* AND YOURSELF?

DO YOU SEE ANY CONNECTION BETWEEN THE WAY PETE COMMUNICATES AND THE WAY HE RELATES TO OTHERS?

IS THERE ANY CONNECTION BETWEEN THE WAY PETE COMMUNICATES AND THE WAY HE SEES HIMSELF?

I think the garden analogy is valid for human interaction; healthy produce flourishes only in the mutually supportive environment. This point of balance is at the heart of the following "modern fairy tale" by psychiatrist Claude Steiner. Don't let the simplicity of this delightful tale fool you. In the garden, the simple truths are the most important to observe. And because they are simple, they are often very hard to see. But they rule the harvest.

BY CLAUDE STEINER
ILLUSTRATIONS BY LYN RINTYE

Once upon a time, a long time ago, there lived two very happy people called Tim and Maggie with two children called John and Lucy. To understand how happy they were, you have to understand how things were in those days.

You see, in those happy days everyone was given at birth a small, soft, Fuzzy Bag. Anytime a person reached into this bag he was able to pull out a Warm Fuzzy.

Warm Fuzzies were very much in demand because whenever somebody was given a Warm Fuzzy it made him feel warm and fuzzy all over. People who didn't get Warm Fuzzies regularly were in danger of developing a sickness in their back which caused them to shrivel up and die.

In those days it was very easy to get Warm Fuzzies. Anytime that somebody felt like it, he might walk up to you and say, "I'd like to have a Warm Fuzzy." You would then reach into your bag and pull out a Fuzzy the size of a little girl's hand. As soon as the Fuzzy saw the light of day it would smile and blossom into a large, shaggy, Warm Fuzzy. You would then lay it on the person's shoulder or head or lap and it would snuggle up and melt right against their skin and make them feel good all over. People were

always asking each other for Warm Fuzzies, and since they were always given freely, getting enough of them was never a problem. There were always plenty to go around and as a consequence everyone felt warm and fuzzy most of the time.

One day a bad witch became angry because everyone was so happy and no one was buying her potions and salves. The witch was very clever and she devised a very wicked plan.

One beautiful morning she crept up to Tim while Maggie was playing with their daughter and whispered in his ear, "See here, Tim, look at all the

Fuzzies that Maggie is giving to Lucy. You know, if she keeps that up, eventually she is going to run out and then there won't be any left for you!"

Tim was astonished. He turned to the witch and said, "Do you mean to tell me that there isn't a Warm Fuzzy in our bag every time we reach into it?" And the witch said, "No, absolutely not, and once you run out . . . that's it. You don't have any more."

With this she flew away on her broom, laughing and cackling hysterically.

Tim took this to heart and began to notice every time Maggie gave up a Warm Fuzzy to somebody else. Eventually he got very worried and upset because he liked Maggie's Warm Fuzzies very much and did not want to give them up. He certainly did not think it was right for Maggie to be spending all her Warm Fuzzies on the children and on other people. He began to complain every time he saw Maggie giving a Warm Fuzzy to somebody else, and because Maggie liked him very much, she stopped giving Warm Fuzzies to other people as often, and reserved them for him.

The children watched this and soon began to get the idea that it was wrong to give up Warm Fuzzies any

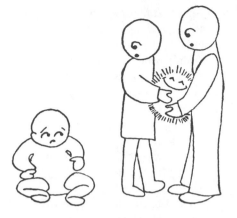

time you were asked or felt like it.
They, too, became very careful. They
would watch their parents closely and
whenever they felt that one of their
parents was giving too many Fuzzies
to others they also began to object.
They began to feel worried whenever
they gave away too many Warm
Fuzzies.

Even though they found a Warm
Fuzzy every time they reached into
their bag, they reached in less and less
and became more and more stingy.
Soon people began to notice the lack
of Warm Fuzzies, and they began to
feel less and less fuzzy. They began to
shrivel up and occasionally, people
would die from lack of Warm Fuzzies.
More and more people went to the

witch to buy her potions and salves
even though they didn't seem to work.

Well, the situation was getting very
serious indeed.

The bad witch who had been
watching all of this didn't really want
the people to die so she devised a new
plan. She gave everyone a bag that was
very similar to the Fuzzy Bag except
that this one was *cold* while the Fuzzy
Bag was warm. Inside of the witch's
bag were Cold Pricklies. These Cold
Pricklies did not make people feel
warm and fuzzy but made them feel
cold and prickly instead. But, they did
prevent peoples' backs from shriveling
up.

So from then on, every time
somebody said, "I want a Warm
Fuzzy," people who were worried
about depleting their supply would
say, "I can't give you a Warm Fuzzy,
but would you like a Cold Prickly?"
Sometimes two people would walk up
to each other, thinking they could get
a Warm Fuzzy, but one or the other of
them would change his mind and they
would wind up giving each other Cold
Pricklies. So, the end result was that
while very few people were dying, a
lot of people were still unhappy and
feeling very cold and prickly.

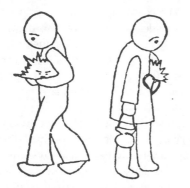

The situation got very complicated because, since the coming of the witch, there were less and less Warm Fuzzies around, so Warm Fuzzies, which used to be thought of as free as air, became extremely valuable. This caused people to do all sorts of things in order to obtain them. Before the witch had appeared, people used to gather in groups of three or four or five, never caring too much who was giving Warm Fuzzies to whom.

After the coming of the witch, people began to pair off and to reserve

all their Warm Fuzzies for each other *exclusively.* If ever one of the two persons forgot himself and gave a Warm Fuzzy to someone else, he would immediately feel guilty about it because he knew that his partner would probably resent the loss of a Warm Fuzzy.

People who could not find a generous partner had to buy their Warm Fuzzies and had to work long hours to earn the money. Another thing which happened was that some people would take Cold Pricklies—which were limitless and freely available—coat them white and fluffy and pass them on as Warm Fuzzies. These counterfeit Warm Fuzzies were really *Plastic Fuzzies,* and they caused

additional difficulties. For instance, two people would get together and freely exchange Plastic Fuzzies, which presumably should make them feel good, but they came away feeling bad instead. Since they thought they had been exchanging Warm Fuzzies, people grew very confused about this, never realizing that their cold prickly feelings were really the result of the fact they had been given a lot of Plastic Fuzzies.

So the situation was very, very dismal and it all started because of the coming of the witch who made people believe that some day, when least expected, they might reach into their Warm Fuzzy Bag and find no more.

Not long ago a young woman with big hips (born under the sign of Aquarius) came to this unhappy land. She had not heard about the bad witch and was not worried about running out of Warm Fuzzies. She gave them out freely, even when not asked. They

called her the Hip Woman and disapproved of her because she was giving the children the idea that they should not worry about running out of Warm Fuzzies. The children liked her very much because they felt good around her and they, too, began to give out Warm Fuzzies whenever they felt like it.

The grown-ups became concerned and decided to pass a law to protect the children from depleting their supplies of Warm Fuzzies. The law made it a criminal offense to give out Warm Fuzzies in a reckless manner. The children, however, seemed not to care, and in spite of the law they continued to give each other Warm Fuzzies whenever they felt like it and always when asked. Because there were many, many children, almost as many as grown-ups, it began to look as if maybe they would have their way.

As of now it is hard to say what will happen.

Will the grown-up forces of law and order stop the recklessness of the children?

Are the grown-ups going to join with the Hip Woman and the children in taking a chance that there will always be as many Warm Fuzzies as needed?

Will they remember the days their children are trying to bring back when Warm Fuzzies were abundant because people gave them away freely?

WHAT DOES THIS FAIRY TALE HAVE TO DO WITH THE WAY
PEOPLE COMMUNICATE?

WHAT IS THE "REAL LIFE" BEHAVIOR REFERRED TO AS A "WARM
FUZZY"?

A "PLASTIC FUZZY"? A "COLD PRICKLY"?

HOW MANY WAYS CAN YOU COMMUNICATE A WARM FUZZY?

DO YOU EVER TRADE COLD PRICKLIES WITH OTHERS?

WHAT ARE YOUR USUAL PLASTIC FUZZY BEHAVIORS?

HOW DOES THIS STORY CONNECT WITH "SUCKER"?

IN WHAT WAY DOES THIS "FUZZY TALE" APPLY TO THE EARLIER
BEHAVIOR YOU SAW IN "THE LISTENER"?

As I read "A Fuzzy Tale," I couldn't help thinking of Ashley
Montagu's book *Touching,* in which he asserts that human beings have a
genuine need for physical touching or stroking. The Tender Loving Care
policies of some hospital nurseries seem to confirm that we people-
types thrive on actual contact with one another: infants touched
frequently by nurses grow faster and develop better than neglected
infants. In a real sense, "A Fuzzy Tale" is saying the same thing, and
extending it into the psychological arena. Mental well-being may be
connected with our personal "contact" with others.

HOW OFTEN DO YOU TRULY "TOUCH" OTHERS?

WHAT KIND OF CONTACTS DO YOU MAKE IN YOUR DAILY
LIFE?

DO YOU SEE ANY CONNECTION BETWEEN THE WAY YOU
DEFINE YOURSELF AND THE WAY YOU CONTACT OTHERS?

To stay with the garden analogy, it seems that "A Fuzzy Tale"
suggests that the healthy garden is characterized by mutual harmony

70   and satisfaction, a giving and taking among the elements that make up the place. And the differences among the elements are what create the balance we feel and smell and see.

In the healthy garden.

But this basic truth of balance, this flowing exchange and mutual tolerance are easily overlooked.

Sometimes, in fact, they are never understood.

Consider the following example, and see if you make any connections between "A Fuzzy Tale" and this short news item from *Newsweek*.

ARIZONA:

Nervously fingering a pink Kleenex, primly smoothing a pair of white gloves in her lap, Mrs. Dorothy Ault sat in the witness chair of an antiquated Phoenix courtroom and told her grisly tale.

The tragedy began, said Mrs. Ault, when she and her husband had awakened early the previous Saturday morning to find their daughter, Linda, still not home from a Friday night at the movies. They searched in vain for the girl throughout nearby Tempe, Ariz., where pretty auburn-haired

Linda was a sophomore studying accounting at Arizona State University. Hours later the girl returned home, her mother said, and cheerfully admitted she had spent the night with an Air Force Officer she knew. "She said she was 21 and what might be wrong for us was all right for her."

SWITCH: Naturally her parents couldn't see it that way. First, Mrs. Ault snatched a mesquite switch from the desert ground and lashed the girl's head. Later that day the Aults withdrew her from the University. Still she was not properly contrite, her mother felt. "I told Linda that after all she had put so many people through and wasn't sorry, maybe she would suffer over an animal," she said. "She loved animals."

And so, next morning, an eerie procession filed out of the modest house on South Mountain to a cactus-dotted gully. With Mr. and Mrs. Ault were Linda and her pet dog, Judy. After they ordered Linda to dig a shallow grave, Mrs. Ault testified, they handed her a newly purchased pistol. "I held the dog and told her 'The best way is through the head.' Linda brought the gun down. Then the gun went back up—I didn't see it any more—and I heard a shot."

Linda Ault died of a gunshot wound in the head. The inquest officially ruled Linda's death a suicide, and stunned authorities at first decided the only charge against the parents could be that of cruelty to animals. But then at the weekend, they arrested the elder Aults on the charge of involuntary manslaughter.

At least, said police Sgt. John Fields, the parents "knew the emotional state of their daughter when they furnished her with a loaded pistol."

HOW MUCH SENSITIVE LISTENING WENT ON IN THIS FAMILY?

DO YOU SEE ANY PARALLEL BETWEEN THE PARENTS' BEHAVIOR AND THAT OF PETE IN "SUCKER"?

WHAT IS THE ROLE OF PUNISHMENT IN A HEALTHY RELATIONSHIP?

It is impossible to cultivate a green thumb in working the human garden unless the rich ground of mutual respect is tilled. Self-respect and respect for others.

DO YOU SEE ANY CONNECTION BETWEEN SELF-DEFINITION AND RESPECT IN RELATING WITH OTHERS?

Of course the word "respect" is loaded, and confusion about its care and feeding is widespread. Psychiatrist R. D. Laing writes of one such "knot" of confusion:

It is the duty of children to respect their parents.
And it is the duty of parents to teach their children
to respect them,
by setting them a good example.

Parents who do not set their children a good example
don't deserve respect.
If we do set them a good example
we believe they will grow up to be grateful to us
when they become parents themselves.

If he is cheeky
he doesn't respect you
for not punishing him
for not respecting you.

You shouldn't spoil a child.
It's the easy way, to do what they want
but they won't respect you for letting them get away
with it when they grow up.

He won't respect you
  if you don't punish him
    for not respecting you.

SEE WHAT I MEAN ABOUT THE WORD "RESPECT"?

When I say that mutual respect is the root base of any growthful human relationship, I am referring to the acceptance of one another— by one another—as different be-ings of humanness. That is, you are and I am.

We are different in many ways, but so is soil different than sunlight than water than insects, etc. Yet *all* are equally necessary, are they not?

There is a principle in Chinese philosophy that might help us understand this notion of symbiotic relationship. It is called "yin-yang," the symbol for which is below.

As the symbol demonstrates, the world is made of positive polarities. That is, for every element in the universe you can define, there is an opposite element.

Another way of saying this is that every "identity" depends upon its opposite to define itself.

For example, imagine "female" without the contrast of "male." Visualize "black" without reference to "white." Define "self" without comparison with "other." "Up" without "down."

Go ahead. Try. Bet you can't come up with *one* definition of anything that does not depend upon comparison, contrast, or reference to its opposite.

I need You to be.

Another point is made by the symbol.

Notice that within the black area is a small bit of white; and within the white area is a small bit of black.

In other words, every element in our universe contains some of its own opposite.

For example, Hitler was kind and gentle to children. Jesus threw moneylenders from the temple, but preached peace. Every kiss is an exchange of infectious bacteria. "You always hurt the one you love." Every "etc." needs a period.

So whatever you are, I am, too—to some extent. We are mutual ground of being.

OUR DIFFERENCES ARE
DELIGHTFULLY ESSENTIAL,
AND OUR SIMILARITIES
MUTUALLY UNAVOIDABLE!

This basic observation about our interdependence is not understood by many persons in our culture, if we can use as our index the behaviors of tolerance and mutual respect. To many individuals, differences among people are not delightful, not essential, not mutual. Instead, differences are frightening, "bad," and entirely avoidable.

"A word to the wise, Benson. People are asking why they don't see Old Glory on your bike."

Perhaps this is true because people forget that human beings have *choice* in how they behave toward one another. And perhaps it's true because once trained in our culture's competitive, carnivore, "win-lose" way of relating to one another, people forget to sit down and listen to

the wisdom of their backyard garden. It could also be true because so
few of us have backyard gardens these days from which to learn the
basic lessons of harmonious relationships.

A more satisfying approach to our interpersonal communion is possible. Healthy relationships do not come in seed packages, but like a
garden effort they do reflect our sense of balance, harmony, and
mutual reverence.

After all, though we do have the privilege of tilling our human
gardens, we do not have access to the secret of *how* the seed of life
germinates. We are merely tenders, caretakers, helpers.

We do not create life.

We *are* life.

And isn't this a wonderful opportunity for the diversity of creatures
who share our plot of ground . . . our ground of being . . . to choose a
full harvest?

An easy beginning might take the form of a question:

Will You Be My Friend?

JAMES KAVANAUGH

Who am I? I am not sure.

Once I was a rabbit's grave and a
basketball hoop on the garage, a
cucumber patch, lilac trees and
peonies crawling with ants. I was
stepping stones and a mysterious
cistern, grass fires, water fights and
ping pong in the basement. I was a
picket fence, a bed and maple chest of
drawers I shared with brothers, a dog
named Sandy who danced. Friends
were easy to find. We climbed trees,
built grass huts, chased snakes—and we
dreamed a lot.
WILL YOU BE MY FRIEND?
Beyond childhood.

Who am I? I am not sure.

Once I was predictable. I was
educated, trained, loved—not as I was,
but as I seemed to be. My role was my
safe way of hiding. There was no
reason to change. I was approved. I
pleased. Then, almost suddenly, I
changed. Now I am less sure, more
myself. My role has almost disappeared. My roots are not in my
church, my job, my city; even my
world. They are in me. Friends are not
so easy to find—and I dream a lot.

WILL YOU BE MY FRIEND?
Beyond roles.

Who am I? I am not sure.

I am more alone than before. Part animal, but not protected by his instincts or restricted by his vision. I am part spirit as well, yet scarcely free, limited by taste and touch and time—yearning for all of life. There is no security. Security is sameness and fear, the postponing of life. Security is expectations and premature death. I live with uncertainty. There are mountains yet to climb, clouds to ride, stars to explore, and friends to find. I am all alone. There is only me—and I dream a lot.

WILL YOU BE MY FRIEND?
Beyond security.

Who am I? I am not sure.

I do not search in emptiness and need, but in increasing fullness and desire. Emptiness seeks any voice to fill a void, any face to dispel darkness. Emptiness brings crowds and shadows easy to replace. Fullness brings a friend, unique, irreplaceable. I am not as empty as I was. There are the wind and the ocean, books and music, strength and joys within, and the night. Friendship is less a request than a celebration, less a ritual than a reality, less a need than a want. Friendship is you and me—and I dream a lot.

WILL YOU BE MY FRIEND?
Beyond need.

Who am I? I am not sure.
Who are you? I want to know.

We didn't sell Kool-Aid together or hitchhike to school. We're not from the same town, the same God, hardly the same world. There is no role to play, no security to provide, no commitment to make. I expect no answer save your presence, your eyes, your self. Friendship is freedom, is flowing, is rare. It does not need stimulation, it stimulates itself. It trusts, understands, grows, explores, it smiles and weeps. It does not exhaust or cling, expect or demand. It is—and that is enough—and it dreams a lot.

WILL YOU BE MY FRIEND?

4

Being
through
Symbols

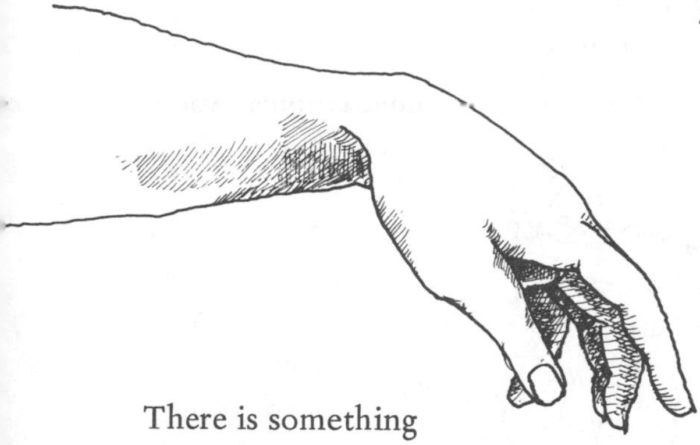

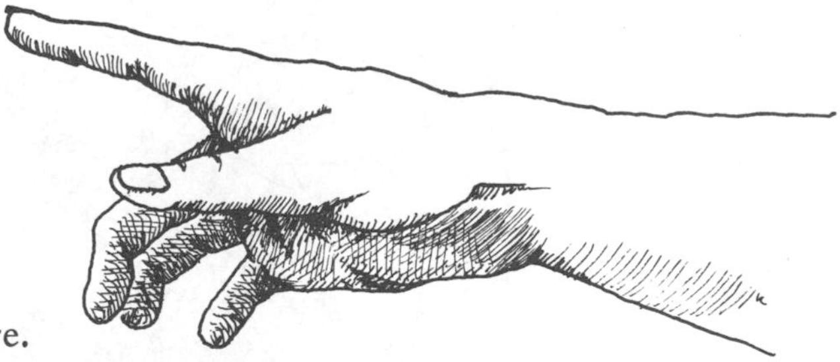

There is something
about being human that
demands reaching out to other
people.

Our need to touch one another, to
be with one another, to understand one
another seems almost biological in nature.
Our need for contact appears to me to go far beyond just our
cultural experience.

This "reaching out" is done largely through symbols. We touch one
another with the fragile tool of language.

And this symbol system is our key to community, to communing, to
communicating.

Because this is true, it is important to understand the nature of symbols and their use.

And to that end this chapter is dedicated.

I guess my starting point in thinking about symbols is the assumption that EVERYONE SEES THE WORLD IN HIS OWN UNIQUE WAY. The realities to which we tie our symbols are often very different.

We are, for example, unique in the animal world. Evolution has given our species special opportunities and special limitations, so that even if we wished to communicate with other creatures, we face the problem of different frameworks.

For instance, have you ever done any scuba diving?

I have. In the waters of the South China Sea.

Those tropical waters were incredible; less than thirty yards offshore where I dived was a reef, which was the feeding site and home of many brilliantly colored tropical fish. They were very gracious creatures, who let me visit their home and families freely. I remember how I admired their sense of community, their friendliness, and their physical beauty and grace.

Although aided by man's latest bubble technology, I was awkward, gurgling frenzy compared with their almost effortless, gliding selves. Their feeding, breathing, and movement were an integrated pattern of energy exchange.

It struck me then how much they knew about the sea that I would never know, because they were fish and I was human. And how much I knew about the sea that they would never know, for the same reason.

Obviously our respective views of "reality" differed.

Or take some other examples.

I cannot hear the silent "whistle" that I use to call my dog. He has the ability to hear a broad spectrum of sound quite beyond my ears. He has hi-fi eardrums.

Consider temperature sensing. I cannot feel heat as sensitively as that female mosquito who hides in my bedroom until dark and then comes out to divebomb my warm flesh. From twelve feet away she can sense my body heat with her antennae and zero in for a feast. Slap!

Nor can I taste as sensitively as the shark, who detects one part blood in one million parts sea water. Can you?

Neither do I smell as sharply as one type of moth, the male being able to pick up female sex spoor from three miles distance. How's *your* nose?

And certainly I do not see as well as the eagle, who can sight food-on-the-hoof from more than a mile aloft. How are your eyes?

MUCH OF THE WORLD GOES BY ME . . . UNSENSED. AND YOU?

More importantly, even among my own kind—other humans—I notice wide differences in sensory abilities. For example, when I learned to fly an airplane I discovered that some people cannot tell green from red. They are "color blind," and don't share my reality when we look at the world. I happen to have 20/20 vision, but my wife wears glasses and cannot identify people more than six feet away with her naked eye. She can smell food burning on the stove when she is in another part of the house, but I cannot. And her nose weeps with sensitivity when grass pollens are in the air, while my nose stays dry.

While physicians talk of "average" or "normal" people, it is plain that such words apply only to the result of arithmetic. Truth is, nobody is exactly the same. Ask your doctor.

REALITY IS DIFFERENT FOR EACH OF US . . . BECAUSE WE SENSE IT WITH DIFFERENT EQUIPMENT.

Leaving now this obvious fact, consider for a moment our *psychological* separateness. Our mental, experiential, emotional differences.

I did not grow up in exactly the same place or time that you did. Nor did I have exactly the same relationship with exactly the same parents as you did.

Neither did we go to the same schools, have the same teachers, nor read the same books at the same speed. Even the way we climbed the monkey bars was different.

We didn't have the same cousins, the same heroes, or the same girl/boy friends. On our summer vacations, as children, I'll bet we didn't ride the same cow, swim the same lake, light the same firecrackers, eat the same berries, or climb the same rocks.

Yet . . . these are the things that shaped our views and attitudes, modeled and tuned our behavior, developed our individual psychological makeup.

And MY PSYCHOLOGICAL MAKEUP STRONGLY INFLUENCES MY PERCEPTION. It is almost as if my internal psychology acts as a screen or grid through which I view the world. As if I tend to see "out there" in the world what is really "in here." I see what I am ready, willing, and able to see. Anything else I tend to ignore, distort to fit my screen, or discredit. Even though many times I may not be aware of the process.

For example, my personality affects what I pay attention to, what is stimulating or boring to me, what I remember and for how long. Recall the earlier articles that dealt with how self-concept influences what I see around me.

We tend to see what we are.

I look at you
and see me.

You look at me
and see you.

However oversimplified, the point is that our psychological characteristics are different, and influence our individual perceptions of reality.

This assumption is critical in thinking about symbols, because symbols are weak tools, indeed, to use in trying to share our differing realities. We must understand the limitations of our tools in tackling such a difficult job.

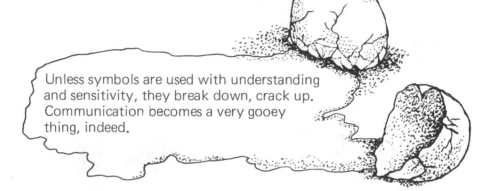

Being a symbol isn't easy. People expect so much of me, yet they usually don't know what I am and what I do.

Frankly, I am getting very tired of trying to meet such unrealistic demands.

Unless symbols are used with understanding and sensitivity, they break down, crack up. Communication becomes a very gooey thing, indeed.

Let me try to define myself here.

I think of a symbol as SOMETHING THAT "STANDS FOR" SOMETHING ELSE. That is, I use symbols to represent some reality I sense, such as a physical object, a feeling, or an idea.

This page, for example.

A sheet of paper covered with hundreds of tiny ink squiggles. Ink squiggles that "stand for" the reality I wish to share with you.

These squiggles (words) have no identity of their own.

They only point to my reality.

They are signposts to my intended meaning.

Another example: Can you read the Japanese squiggle you see opposite?

A squiggle is a squiggle.

Actually, it points to the reality we call "bliss" or "enjoyment."

Doesn't really matter which squiggle we use, does it, as long as we understand the reality intended?

Of course, we must *know* the link between the symbol and the reality represented, or we miss the meaning intended.

But to truly understand this link between symbol and reality, we must recognize a third element. Always present. Usually ignored.

I speak of the MIND OF THE USER.

After all, *someone* symbols something.

Another way of saying this is: "Meaning" is a relationship between the elements of a symbol, user, and reality. There is never a direct connection between a symbol and a reality, except as that connection is established through the mind of the symbol user.

USER'S MIND

SYMBOL . . . REALITY

SYMBOLS HAVE NO MEANING;
ONLY PEOPLE HAVE MEANING.

Even as I sit in front of my typewriter, writing this sentence, I am aware that when you read it we will be doing nothing more than "symbol swapping." With no check on whether or not our triangles of meaning overlap.

As long as we are aware of this foolish reality, and don't take ourselves too seriously, perhaps we needn't be upset.

But most people I know speak, write, listen, and read just as if *everyone used symbols the same way.*

84

In fact, as you read this right now, are you making this common
error?

FIREFLIES

IS A "COMMON LANGUAGE" ENOUGH?

For myself, it is one thing to realize intellectually that symbol
"meaning" depends entirely upon the user, and quite another thing to
change my old symbol behaviors. I was raised to believe that words had
meaning. I used to run to a dictionary for meaning, whenever I heard
someone use a new word. DID YOU?

Even today, after several years of knowing better, I still find myself
slipping back into my childhood view of language . . . that there is a
direct connection between a symbol and its reality. I know better, intellectually, but I often behave as if I did not. Let me give you an
example.

Last week I went shopping at a local produce market that advertises their produce as "home grown." Since I have a modest garden myself, I knew what "home grown" meant, so I filled my basket with fresh melons and fruit.

The family that owns and operates the market is Japanese-American, and I stopped to talk with one of the older family members about how he grew his produce.

He led me to the rear of the store and waved his arm out the window toward several acres of crop-covered land. I could see a dozen or more workers driving tractors, operating a large irrigation system, and planting. One man near me was spreading insecticide dust over silk-topped corn ears.

Next to the cornfield was a large patch of melons, with several mounds of giant plants.

Also covered with toxic pesticide.

"Home growing" away!

Somehow that poisoned reality and the words "home grown" didn't fit together in my head. I had *assumed* that "home grown" meant the farmer used organic growing methods, and I had filled my basket with poisoned fruit just as if the symbol was the reality. My reality.

Fortunately I stumbled onto the market owner's meaning before I ate my mistake and fed my family that toxic food.

A general semanticist would express the lesson I relearned a different way. He might use the phrase "The map is not the territory." As a word only stands for a reality, so a map only stands for a territory. If the map is out of date, inaccurately drawn or labeled, then you're in trouble. But even if it is accurate and up to date, it is only a map—not the territory itself. In my market behavior, I had mistaken the map for the territory.

I remember that a few years ago in Viet Nam I experienced a literal example of this problem. During one operation some men of my company were to accompany a combat patrol into unknown territory. The map we had showed a river route covered by dense brush. Excellent terrain feature for concealment of the patrol as it advanced toward the objective. Only trouble was, once the patrol reached the river position they discovered that there was no river nor any concealing brush. The map turned out to be a copy of an earlier French version, and I later learned that the river had existed and been recorded some forty years before! Can you imagine the patrol leader's comment?

That's right.

He calmly said . . . "Men, this is a wonderful lesson in general semantics, isn't it?"

Sure he did.

"Home grown" and "river brush" are both traps, if you believe that my symbol represents your reality, or vice versa.

THE SYMBOL IS NOT REALITY.

THE WORD IS NOT THE THING.

THE MAP IS NOT THE TERRITORY.

One final point I want to make on the nature of symbols as sharing tools: some symbols are more precise "pointers" than others.

Do you remember your English teachers in school talking about words that were "general" and other words that were "concrete"? That's the distinction I want to get at here. You might find it fun to glance at some newspaper headlines and try to visualize the reality intended by the words used.

Peru Reels as Anchovy Crisis Persists

Tight Money Ahead, U.S. Survey Says

Navy Studies Morale Effect on Health

China Youth Shun Politics, Russia Says

Governmental Lag on Sex Bias

Have you ever seen "tight money" or a "governmental lag"?

So-called concrete words generally point to some part of the physical world. They are "reporting words" that stand for something I see, taste, smell, hear, or touch. For example:

> "Four-month-old Siberian tiger"
> "One-inch steel ball-bearing"
> "A twelve-ounce glass tumbler"

General semanticists refer to such words as "low-level abstractions." That is, there are fewer meanings likely to be attached to them than to "general" words, also called "high-level abstractions."

"General" words often confuse, because they point to conclusions or inferences rather than physical fact. People have more room for interpretation. For example, notice how the creature pictured opposite becomes more difficult to pin down as the words used to describe him become increasingly abstract.

Youthful cat

Young tiger

Tiger cub

Four-month-old
Siberian tiger

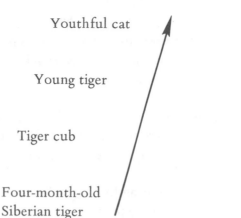

If you were told that the elderly lady next door spent her time playing with a "youthful cat," you might imagine anything from a middle-aged swinger to an aging Siamese house cat on hormone shots.

It surprises me how much daily conversation is made up of high-level abstractions. Eavesdropping on a few conversations, I picked up these examples:

> "I'm not *smart,* but I'm not *dumb,* either."
> "She *treats everyone that way.*"
> "We're *active club people.*"
> "*College* just isn't *real life.*"
> "I *want* to *do something worthwhile in life.*"
> "*Treat* him *right* and he'll *do the same.*"
> "That's a *good attitude* to *have.*"

I find it difficult to have confidence in my interpretation of any of these phrases, because they are all composed of symbols at a high level of abstraction.

If you want to persuade, of course, high-level abstractions can be used effectively. For example, here is an excerpt from a U.S. Army recruiting pamphlet:

90   Field Artillery. The power punch of the Army's combat specialties. To give support to ground troops. To break up and delay enemy attacks. Often the difference between success and failure.

Not one low-level word about splintered bones or bloody body meat, which are the concrete reality of artillery fire. Here's another example from an investment concern:

Outstanding financial opportunity due to aggressive dollar management.

Base your future on that reality, if you dare. The reason these high-level abstractions are effective in persuading is that they allow the listener/reader to tag his own reality to them. And it is for this very reason that they are not effective for accurate sharing, for trading/matching realities.

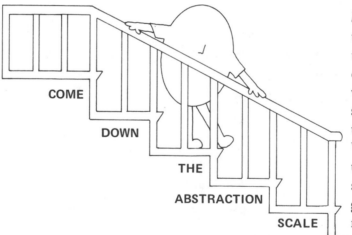

COME

DOWN

THE

ABSTRACTION

SCALE

Obviously the *lower* the abstraction level used, the greater the chance that we will be able to share our individual realities. When speaking, use words that stay close to the ground, right next to what you want to point to.

For example, don't say that "Father is mad," but that "He shouted at me." Not that "You have never liked me," but that "You have never invited me to your house." When you are listening, you can be helpful in getting the speaker down the abstraction scale by asking questions that call for definite, factual answers. Here are some examples I use:

1. How do you know that?

2. What did you see?

3. When did it happen?

4. Where?

5. Who was there?

6. How did you behave?

> WHEN YOU SPEAK AND WHEN YOU LISTEN . . USE WORDS YOU CAN TOUCH, SMELL, TASTE, HEAR, AND SEE

By the way, some speakers are "bugged" when they are questioned. They feel questioning is a challenge to their truthfulness, and they become defensive.

So feel your way slowly.

WHERE

DOES

THIS

LEAD

US?

Looking back now at my earlier definition of "symbol," and at some of the implications discussed, one conclusion seems unavoidable.

WE CANNOT TAKE SYMBOL COMMUNICATION FOR
GRANTED.

It is apparent that even the most articulate
person must bow to the "reality" that symbols are weak tools for the heavy job expected of them.

I believe that many so-called communication problems are, in fact, frustrations caused
by unrealistic expectations. People throw
themselves off-center by regarding symbols as
accurate, precise devices, instead of understanding the essential ambiguity of any sym-
bol. From these people I hear such statements as "I understood him
perfectly, didn't you?" and "Don't you understand English?" Another
favorite is "But I said that before!" Just as if meaning was in words,
and everyone made the same connection between certain words and
certain realities. A nonsense position.

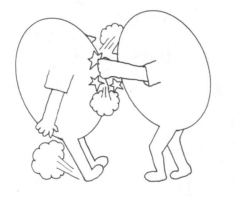

Having done this . . .

A far more balanced posture
is one in which we do our best
to use concrete symbols, and
whenever possible *show* our
listener the physical reality we
speak of. Follow this up by
seeking some form of feedback
from him, to check on his understanding of our message.

EXPECT INACCURACY;

EXPECT INCOMPLETENESS;

EXPECT MISUNDERSTANDING.

Expect very limited success.

Avoid "locking-in" on one interpretation of anything we hear.

And give up the luxury and security of a false impression of the nature and use of symbols.

DO YOU SEE THE IMPORTANCE OF GOODWILL HERE?

In using such flimsy tools, can you imagine attempting to share your meaning with someone who will not make a genuine effort himself? Someone who refuses to remain open, patient, and tentative in interpreting your symbols? Someone who thinks he knows what you mean, even before you have finished speaking? Such an attempt is doomed from the start.

Symbol sharing is a fragile enterprise.

We touch with very tentative fingers.

By its very nature, human communication requires *mutual* commitment and care. We are invited to make an art of our sharing, since nothing less will work.

In one sense, then, there is a moral imperative in the limitations of human communication. An imperative prompting patience, tolerance, and goodwill.

And in this sense, our limitations become our opportunities.

You are correct if you see implications in this conclusion for other areas of daily life. Balance in one part of life often has a settling, centering influence on other parts.

> TO ACHIEVE HUMAN COMMUNICATION
> IS TO MAKE OF LIFE AN ART

5

Being
without
Words

Last summer I decided that I wanted a water fountain in my front yard.

Not the kind you buy, already put together, but a rock running, moss covering, trickle gurgle pleasure.

So I created one.

And it still surprises me how many people stop as they pass, to stand for minutes looking into the pool and listening to the splashing speech of falling water.

Hundreds of thousands of years of human evolution stand there in communion.

When they walk away, they seem calmer.

96   Something has been communicated.

I doubt they could express in words what's happened, but the message of those quiet moments has been meaningful.

Each time I see this I am reminded that much in life is communicated without words. Not only between man and the rest of nature, but between men themselves.

In fact, I would bet that *most* of my communication is nonverbally expressed/received. Probably only about 20% of my symboling is verbal (words). The remaining 80% is wordless.

WHAT IS YOUR ESTIMATE?

It's not surprising when I stop to think about it. Man has been a nonverbal creature most of his time on earth. It's only in the last several thousand years that words have been developed. My fantasy is that man has survived because he could read well the nonverbal cues of his world.

And to the degree he retains and uses that skill today, he will continue to survive.

What *is* surprising to me is that many people think of nonverbal communication solely in relation to "body language." To me, body language is only *one* nonverbal vocabulary.

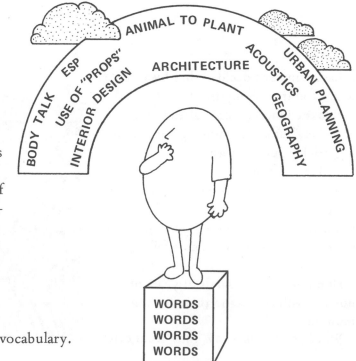

There are dozens.

What I would like to do in this chapter is suggest to you some of those vocabularies. Mostly through the writings of others, I want to explore with you the *variety* in symbol/signal systems.

Let's begin with body language, and then move into some areas not usually thought of as communication systems.

Our first article, from *Playboy* Magazine, is written by Ed Hall, a cultural anthropologist and pioneer in exploring nonverbal behavior, and his wife, Mildred. They focus on the nonverbal cues of posture, gesture, facial expression, costume, the way we walk, even our treatment of time and space and material things.

Somewhere in this article, I bet that you catch a glimpse of your own behavior.

THE SOUNDS
OF SILENCE

Bob leaves his apartment at 8:15 a.m. and stops at the corner drugstore for breakfast. Before he can speak, the counterman says, "The usual?" Bob nods yes. While he savors his Danish, a fat man pushes onto the adjoining stool and overflows into his space. Bob scowls and pulls himself in as much as he can. Bob has sent two messages without speaking a syllable.

Henry has an appointment to meet Arthur at 11 o'clock; he arrives at 11:30. Their conversation is friendly, but Arthur retains a lingering hostility. Henry has unconsciously communicated that he doesn't think the appointment is very important or that Arthur is a person who needs to be treated with respect.

George is talking to Charley's wife at a party. Their conversation is entirely trivial, yet Charley glares at them suspiciously. Their physical proximity and the movements of their eyes reveal that they are powerfully attracted to each other.

José Ybarra and Sir Edmund Jones are at the same party and it is important for them to establish a cordial relationship for business reasons. Each is trying to be warm and friendly, yet they will part with mutual distrust and their business transaction will probably fall through. José, in Latin fashion, moved closer and closer to Sir Edmund as they spoke, and this movement was miscommunicated as push-

ing to Sir Edmund, who kept backing away from this intimacy, and this was miscommunicated to José as coldness. The silent languages of Latin and English cultures are more difficult to learn than their spoken languages.

In each of these cases, we see the subtle power of nonverbal communication. The only language used throughout most of the history of humanity (in evolutionary terms, vocal communication is relatively recent), it is the first form of communication you learn. You use this preverbal language, consciously and unconsciously, everyday to tell other people how you feel about yourself and them.

This language includes your posture, gestures, facial expressions, costume, the way you walk, even your treatment of time and space and material things. All people communicate on several different levels at the same time but are usually aware of only the verbal dialog and don't realize that they respond to nonverbal messages. But when a person says one thing and really believes something else, the discrepancy between the two can usually be sensed. Nonverbal communication systems are much less subject to the conscious deception that often occurs in verbal systems. When we find ourselves thinking, "I don't know what it is about him, but he doesn't seem sincere," it's usually this lack of congruity between a person's words and his behavior that makes us anxious and uncomfortable.

Few of us realize how much we all depend on body movement in our

conversation or are aware of the hidden rules that govern listening behavior. But we know instantly whether or not the person we're talking to is "tuned in" and we're very sensitive to any breach in listening etiquette. In white middle-class American culture, when someone wants to show he is listening to someone else, he looks either at the other person's face or, specifically, at his eyes, shifting his gaze from one eye to the other.

You use this preverbal language, consciously and unconsciously, everyday to tell other people how you feel about yourself and about them.

If you observe a person conversing, you'll notice that he indicates he's listening by nodding his head. He also makes little "Hmm" noises. If he agrees with what's being said, he may give a vigorous nod. To show pleasure or affirmation, he smiles; if he has some reservations, he looks skeptical by raising an eyebrow or pulling down the corners of his mouth. If a participant wants to terminate the conversation, he may start shifting his body position, stretching his legs, crossing or uncrossing them, bobbing his foot or diverting his gaze from the speaker. The more he fidgets, the more the speaker becomes aware that he has lost his audience. As a last measure, the listener may look at his watch to indicate the imminent end of the conversation.

Talking and listening are so intricately intertwined that a person cannot do one without the other. Even when one is alone and talking to oneself, there is part of the brain that speaks while another part listens. In all conversations, the listener is positively or negatively reinforcing the speaker all the time. He may even guide the conversation without knowing it, by laughing or frowning or dismissing the argument with a wave of his hand.

The language of the eyes—another age-old way of exchanging feelings—is both subtle and complex. Not only do men and women use their eyes differently but there are class, generation, regional, ethnic and national cultural differences. Americans often complain about the way foreigners stare at people or hold a glance too long. Most Americans look away from someone who is using his eyes in an unfamiliar way because it makes them self-conscious. If a man looks at another man's wife in a certain way, he's asking for trouble, as indicated earlier. But he might not be ill mannered or seeking to challenge the husband. He might be a European in this country who hasn't learned our visual mores. Many American women visiting France or Italy are acutely embarrassed because, for the first time in their lives, men really look at them—their eyes, hair, nose, lips, breasts, hips, legs, thighs, knees, ankles, feet, clothes, hairdo, even their walk. These same women, once they have become used to being looked at, often return to the United States and are overcome with the feeling that "No one ever really looks at me anymore."

Analyzing the mass of data on the eyes, it is possible to sort out at least three ways in which the eyes are used to communicate: dominance vs. submission, involvement vs. detachment, and positive vs. negative attitude. In addition, there are three levels of consciousness and control, which can be categorized as follows: (1) conscious use of the eyes to communicate, such as the flirting blink and the intimate nose-wrinkling squint; (2) the very extensive category of unconscious but learned behavior governing where the eyes are directed and when (this unwritten set of rules dictates how and under what circumstances the sexes, as well as people of all status categories, look at each other); and (3) the response of the eye itself, which is completely outside both awareness and control—changes in the cast (the sparkle) of the eye and the pupillary reflex.

The eye is unlike any other organ of the body, for it is an extension of the brain. The unconscious pupillary reflex and the cast of the eye have been known by people of Middle Eastern origin for years—although most are unaware of their knowledge. Depending on the context, Arabs and others look either directly at the eyes or deeply *into* the eyes of their interlocutor. We became aware of this in the Middle East several years ago while looking at jewelry. The merchant suddenly started to push a particular bracelet at a customer and said, "You buy this one." What interested us was that the bracelet was not the one that had been consciously selected by the purchaser. But the merchant, watching the pupils of the eyes, knew what the purchaser really wanted to buy. Whether he specifically knew *how* he knew is debatable.

A psychologist at the University of Chicago, Eckhard Hess, was the first to conduct systematic studies of the pupillary reflex. His wife remarked one evening, while watching him reading in bed, that he must be very interested in the text because his pupils were dilated. Following up on this, Hess slipped some pictures of nudes into a stack of photographs that he gave to his male assistant. Not looking at the photographs but watching his assistant's pupils, Hess was able to tell precisely when the assistant came to the nudes. In further experiments, Hess retouched the eyes in a photograph of a woman. In one print, he made the pupils small, in another, large; nothing else was changed. Subjects who were given the photographs found the woman with the dilated pupils much more attractive. Any man who has had the experience of seeing a woman look at him as her pupils widen with reflex speed knows that she's flashing him a message.

The eye-sparkle phenomenon frequently turns up in our interviews of couples in love. It's apparently one of the first reliable clues in the other person that love is genuine. To date, there is no scientific data to explain eye sparkle; no investigation of the pupil, the cornea or even the white sclera of the eye shows how the sparkle originates. Yet we all know it when we see it.

One common situation for most people involves the use of the eyes in the street and in public. Although eye behavior follows a definite set of rules, the rules vary according to the place, the needs and feelings of the people, and their ethnic background. For urban whites, once they're within definite recognition distance (sixteen to thirty-two feet for people with average eyesight), there is mutual avoidance of eye contact—unless they want something specific: a pickup, a handout or information of some kind. In the West and in small towns generally, however, people are much more likely to look at and greet one another, even if they're strangers.

It's permissible to look at people if they're beyond recognition distance; but once inside this sacred zone, you can only steal a glance at strangers. You *must* greet friends, however; to fail to do so is insulting. Yet, to stare too fixedly even at them is considered rude and hostile. Of course, all these rules are variable.

A great many blacks, for example, greet each other in public even if they don't know each other. To blacks, most eye behavior of whites has the effect of giving the impression that they aren't there, but this is due to white avoidance of eye contact with *anyone* in the street.

Another very basic difference between people of different ethnic background is their sense of territoriality and how they handle space. This is the silent communication, or miscommunication, that caused friction between Mr. Ybarra and Sir Edmund Jones in our earlier example. We know from research that everyone has around himself an invisible bubble of space that contracts and expands depending on several factors: his emotional state, the activity he's performing at the time and his cultural background. This bubble is a kind of mobile territory that he will defend against intrusion. If he is accustomed to close personal distance between himself and others, his bubble will be smaller than that of someone who's

accustomed to greater personal distance. People of North European heritage—English, Scandinavian, Swiss and German—tend to avoid contact. Those whose heritage is Italian, French, Spanish, Russian, Latin American or Middle Eastern like close personal contact.

People are very sensitive to any intrusion into their spatial bubble. If someone stands too close to you, your first instinct is to back up. If that's not possible, you lean away and pull yourself in, tensing your muscles. If the intruder doesn't respond to these body signals, you may then try to protect yourself, using a briefcase, umbrella or raincoat. Women—especially when traveling alone—often plant their pocketbook in such a way that no one can get very close to them. As a last resort, you may move to another spot and position yourself behind a desk or a chair that provides screening.

Everyone tries to adjust the space around himself in a way that's comfortable for him; most often, he does this unconsciously.

Emotions also have a direct effect on the size of a person's territory. When you're angry or under stress, your bubble expands and you require

more space. New York psychiatrist Augustus Kinzel found a difference in what he calls Body Buffer Zones between violent and non-violent prison inmates. Dr. Kinzel conducted experiments in which each prisoner was placed in the center of a small room and then Dr. Kinzel slowly walked toward him. Nonviolent prisoners allowed him to come quite close, while prisoners with a history of violent behavior couldn't tolerate his proximity and reacted with some vehemence.

Apparently, people under stress experience other people as looming larger and closer than they actually are.

Studies of schizophrenic patients have indicated that they sometimes have a distorted perception of space, and several psychiatrists have reported patients who experience their body boundaries as filling up an entire room. For these patients, anyone who comes into the room is actually inside their body, and such an intrusion may trigger a violent outburst.

Unfortunately, there is little detailed information about normal people who live in highly congested urban areas. We do know, of course, that the noise, pollution, dirt, crowding and confusion of our cities induce feelings of stress in most of us, and stress leads to a need for greater space. The man who's packed into a subway, jostled in the street, crowded into an elevator and forced to work all day in a bull pen or in a small office without auditory or visual privacy is going to be very stressed at the end of his day.

He needs places that provide relief from constant overstimulation of his nervous system. Stress from overcrowding is cumulative and people can tolerate more crowding early in the day than later; note the increased bad temper during the evening rush hour as compared with the morning melee. Certainly one factor in people's desire to commute by car is the need for privacy and relief from crowding (except, often, from other cars); it may be the only time of the day when nobody can intrude.

In crowded public places, we tense our muscles and hold ourselves stiff, and thereby communicate to others our desire not to intrude on their space and, above all, not to touch them. We also avoid eye contact, and the total effect is that of someone who has "tuned out." Walking along the street, our bubble expands slightly as we move in a stream of strangers, taking care not to bump into them. In the office, at meetings, in restaurants, our bubble keeps changing as it adjusts to the activity at hand.

Most white middle-class Americans use four main distances in their business and social relations: intimate, personal, social and public. Each of these distances has a near and a far phase and is accompanied by changes in the volume of the voice. Intimate distance varies from direct physical contact with another person to a distance of six to eighteen inches and is used for our most private activities —caressing another person or making love. At this distance, you are overwhelmed by sensory inputs from the

---

Most white middle-class Americans use four main distances in their business and social relations: intimate, personal, social and public.

---

other person—heat from the body, tactile stimulation from the skin, the fragrance of perfume, even the sound of breathing—all of which literally envelop you. Even at the far phase, you're still within easy touching distance. In general, the use of intimate distance in public between adults is frowned on. It's also much too close for strangers, except under conditions of extreme crowding.

In the second zone—personal distance—the close phase is one and a half to two and a half feet; it's at this distance that wives usually stand from their husbands in public. If another woman moves into this zone, the wife will most likely be disturbed. The far phase—two and a half to four feet—is the distance used to "keep someone at arm's length" and is the most common spacing used by people in conversation.

The third zone—social distance—is employed during business transactions or exchanges with a clerk or repairman. People who work together tend to use close social distance—four to seven feet. This is also the distance for conversation at social gatherings. To stand at this distance from someone who is seated has a dominating effect (e.g., teacher to pupil, boss to secretary). The far phase of the third zone —seven to twelve feet—is where people stand when someone says, "Stand back so I can look at you." This distance lends a formal tone to business or social discourse. In an executive office, the desk serves to keep people at this distance.

The fourth zone—public distance —is used by teachers in classrooms or speakers at public gatherings. At its farthest phase—twenty-five feet and beyond—it is used for important public figures. Violations of this distance can lead to serious complications. During his 1970 U.S. visit, the president of France, Georges Pompidou, was harassed by pickets in Chicago, who were permitted to get within touching distance. Since pickets

in France are kept behind barricades a block or more away, the president was outraged by this insult to his person, and President Nixon was obliged to communicate his concern as well as offer his personal apologies.

It is interesting to note how American pitchmen and panhandlers exploit the unwritten, unspoken conventions of eye and distance. Both take advantage of the fact that once explicit eye contact is established, it is rude to look away, because to do so means to brusquely dismiss the other person and his needs. Once having caught the eye of his mark, the panhandler then locks on, not letting go until he moves through the public zone, the social zone, the personal zone and, finally, into the intimate sphere, where people are most vulnerable.

Touch also is an important part of the constant stream of communication that takes place between people. A light touch, a firm touch, a blow, a caress are all communications. In an effort to break down barriers among people, there's been a recent upsurge in group-encounter activities, in which strangers are encouraged to touch one another. In special situations such as these, the rules for not touching are broken with group approval and people gradually lose some of their inhibitions.

Although most people don't realize it, space is perceived and distances are set not by vision alone but with all the senses. Auditory space is perceived with the ears, thermal space with the skin, kinesthetic space with the muscles of the body and olfactory space with the nose.

distance between people in the third and fourth generations of some families, despite their prolonged contact with people of very different cultural heritages.

Whenever there is great cultural distance between two people, there are bound to be problems arising from differences in behavior and expectations. An example is the American couple who consulted a psychiatrist about their marital problems. The husband was from New England and had been brought up by reserved parents who taught him to control his

> *It is becoming clear to me that I see and hear with my entire body. The tensions in my stomach and back, the position of my head, the movements of my limbs, all affect the quality of my perception. If my legs are crossed and I open them, if I am leaning intently forward and I lean gently back, if my face is tight and I let the muscles go, then a small but measurable change takes place in all the sights and sounds around me.*
>
> HUGH PRATHER
> *I Touch the Earth,
> the Earth Touches Me*

And, once again, it's one's culture that determines how his senses are programmed—which sensory information ranks highest and lowest. The important thing to remember is that culture is very persistent. In this country, we've noted the existence of culture patterns that determine

emotions and to respect the need for privacy. His wife was from an Italian family and had been brought up in close contact with all the members of her large family, who were extremely warm, volatile and demonstrative.

When the husband came home after a hard day at the office, dragging his feet and longing for peace and quiet, his wife would rush to him and smother him. Clasping his hands, rubbing his brow, crooning over his weary head, she never left him alone. But when the wife was upset or anxious about her day, the husband's response was to withdraw completely and leave her alone. No comforting, no affectionate embrace, no attention— just solitude. The woman became convinced her husband didn't love her and, in desperation, she consulted a psychiatrist. Their problem wasn't basically psychological but cultural.

Why has man developed all these different ways of communicating messages without words? One reason is that people don't like to spell out certain kinds of messages. We prefer to find other ways of showing our feelings. This is especially true in relationships as sensitive as courtship. Men don't like to be rejected and most women don't want to turn a man down bluntly. Instead, we work out subtle ways of encouraging or discouraging each other that save face and avoid confrontations.

How a person handles space in dating others is an obvious and very sensitive indicator of how he or she feels about the other person. On a first date, if a woman sits or stands so close to a man that he is acutely conscious of her physical presence—inside the intimate zone—the man usually construes it to mean that she is encouraging him. However, before the

man starts moving in on the woman, he should be sure what message she's really sending; otherwise, he risks bruising his ego. What is close to someone of North European background may be neutral or distant to someone of Italian heritage. Also, women sometimes use space as a way of misleading a man and there are few things that put men off more than women who communicate contradictory messages—such as women who cuddle up and then act insulted when a man takes the next step.

How does a woman communicate interest in a man? In addition to such

familiar gambits as smiling at him, she may glance shyly at him, blush and then look away. Or she may give him a real come-on look and move in very close when he approaches. She may touch his arm and ask for a light. As she leans forward to light her cigarette, she may brush him lightly, enveloping him in her perfume. She'll probably continue to smile at him and she may use what ethologists call preening

*How does a woman
communicate interest
in a man?*

gestures—touching the back of her hair, thrusting her breasts forward, tilting her hips as she stands or crossing her legs if she's seated, perhaps even exposing one thigh or putting a hand on her thigh and stroking it. She may also stroke her wrists as she converses or show the palm of her hand as a way of gaining his attention. Her skin may be unusually flushed or quite pale, her eyes brighter, the pupils larger.

If a man sees a woman whom he wants to attract, he tries to present himself by his posture and stance as someone who is self-assured. He moves briskly and confidently. When he catches the eye of the woman, he may hold her glance a little longer than normal. If he gets an encouraging smile, he'll move in close and engage her in small talk. As they converse, his glance shifts over her face and body. He, too, may make preening gestures —straightening his tie, smoothing his hair or shooting his cuffs.

How do people learn body language? The same way they learn spoken language—by observing and imitating people around them as they're growing up. Little girls imitate their mothers or an older female. Little boys imitate their fathers or a respected uncle or a character on television. In this way, they learn the gender signals appropriate for their sex. Regional, class and ethnic patterns of body behavior are also learned in childhood and persist throughout life.

*How do people learn
body language?*

Such patterns of masculine and feminine body behavior vary widely from one culture to another. In America, for example, women stand with their thighs together. Many walk with their pelvis tipped slightly forward and their upper arms close to their body. When they sit, they cross their legs at the knee or, if they are well past middle age, they may cross their ankles. American men hold their arms away from their body, often swinging them as they walk. They stand with their legs apart (an extreme example is the cowboy, with legs apart and thumbs tucked into his belt). When they sit, they put their feet on the floor with legs apart and, in some parts of the country, they cross their legs by putting one ankle on the other knee.

Leg behavior indicates sex, status and personality. It also indicates whether or not one is at ease or is showing respect or disrespect for the other person. Young Latin American males avoid crossing their legs. In their world of *machismo*, the preferred position for young males when with one another (if there is no older dominant male present to whom they must show respect) is to sit on the base of their spine with their leg muscles relaxed and their feet wide apart. Their respect position is like our military equivalent; spine straight, heels and ankles together—almost identical to that displayed by properly brought up young women in New England in the early part of this century.

American women who sit with their legs spread apart in the presence of males are *not* normally signaling a come-on—they are simply (and often unconsciously) sitting like men. Middle-class women in the presence of other women to whom they are very close may on occasion throw themselves down on a soft chair or sofa and let themselves go. This is a signal that nothing serious will be taken up. Males, on the other hand, lean back and prop their legs up on the nearest object.

The way we walk, similarly, indicates status, respect, mood and ethnic or cultural affiliation. The many variants of the female walk are too well known to go into here, except to say that a man would have to be blind

---

Leg behavior indicates sex, status, personality and respect or disrespect.

---

not to be turned on by the way some women walk—a fact that made Mae West rich before scientists ever studied these matters. To white Americans, some French middle-class males walk in a way that is both humorous and suspect. There is a bounce and looseness to the French walk, as though the parts of the body were somehow unrelated. Jacques Tati, the French movie actor, walks this way; so does the great mime, Marcel Marceau.

Blacks and whites in America— with the exception of middle and upper-middle-class professionals of both groups—move and walk very differently from each other. To the blacks, whites often seem incredibly stiff, almost mechanical in their movements. Black males, on the other hand, have a looseness and coordination that frequently makes whites a little uneasy; it's too different, too integrated, too alive, too male. Norman Mailer has said that squares walk from the shoulders, like bears, but blacks and hippies walk from the hips, like cats.

All over the world, people walk not only in their own characteristic way but have walks that communicate the nature of their involvement with whatever it is they're doing. The

inhabitants even had a name for the respectful walk that one used when in the presence of a chief or when walking past a chief's house. The term was *sufan*, which meant to be humble and respectful.

Only in recent years, however, have scientists begun to make systematic observations of body motions. Ray L. Birdwhistell of the University of Pennsylvania is one of the pioneers in body-motion research and coined the term *kinesics* to describe this field. He developed an elaborate notation system to record both facial and body movements, using an approach similar to that of the linguist, who studies the basic elements of speech. Birdwhistell

> The notion that people communicate volumes by their gestures, facial expressions, posture and walk is not new; actors, dancers, writers and psychiatrists have long been aware of it.

purposeful walk of North Europeans is an important component of proper behavior on the job. Any male who has been in the military knows how essential it is to walk properly (which makes for a continuing source of tension between blacks and whites in the Service). The quick shuffle of servants in the Far East in the old days was a show of respect. On the island of Truk, when we last visited, the and other kinesicists such as Albert Sheflen, Adam Kendon and William Condon take movies of people interacting. They run the film over and over again, often at reduced speed for frame-by-frame analysis, so that they can observe even the slightest body movements not perceptible at normal interaction speeds. These movements are then recorded in notebooks for later analysis.

To appreciate the importance of nonverbal-communication systems, consider the unskilled inner-city black looking for a job. His handling of time and space alone is sufficiently different from the white middle-class pattern to create great misunderstandings on both sides. The black is told to appear for a job interview at a certain time. He arrives late. The white interviewer concludes from his tardy arrival that the black is irresponsible and not really interested in the job. What the interviewer doesn't know is that the black time system (often referred to by blacks as C.P.T.—colored people's time) isn't the same as that of whites. In the words of a black student who had been told to make an appointment to see his professor: "Man, you *must* be putting me on. I never had an appointment in my life."

The black job applicant, having arrived late for his interview, may further antagonize the white interviewer by his posture and his eye behavior. Perhaps he slouches and avoids looking at the interviewer; to him, this is playing it cool. To the interviewer, however, he may well look shifty and sound uninterested. The interviewer has failed to notice the actual signs of interest and eagerness in the black's behavior, such as the subtle shift in the quality of the voice—a gentle and tentative excitement—an almost imperceptible change in the cast of the eyes and a relaxing of the jaw muscles.

Moreover, correct reading of black-white behavior is continually complicated by the fact that both groups are comprised of individuals—some of whom try to accommodate and some of whom make it a point of pride *not* to accommodate.

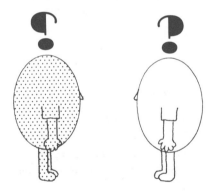

At present, this means that many Americans, when thrown into contact with one another, are in the precarious position of not knowing which pattern applies. Once identified and analyzed, nonverbal-communication systems can be taught, like a foreign language. Without this training, we respond to nonverbal communications in terms of our own culture; we read everyone's behavior as if it were our own, and thus we often misunderstand it.

Several years ago in New York City, there was a program for sending children from predominantly black and Puerto Rican low-income neighborhoods to summer school in a white upper-class neighborhood on the East Side. One morning, a group of young black and Puerto Rican boys raced down the street, shouting and screaming and overturning garbage cans on their way to school. A doorman from an apartment building nearby chased them and cornered one of them inside a building. The boy drew a knife and attacked the doorman. This tragedy would not have occurred if the doorman had been familiar with the behavior of boys from low-income neighborhoods, where such antics are routine and socially acceptable and where pursuit would be expected to invite a violent response.

Nonverbal communication can be taught, but without this training, we read everyone's behavior as if it were our own.

The language of behavior is extremely complex. Most of us are lucky to have under control one subcultural system—the one that reflects our sex, class, generation and geographic region within the United States. Because of its complexity, efforts to isolate bits of nonverbal communication and generalize from them are in vain; you don't become an instant expert on people's behavior by watching them at cocktail parties. Body language isn't something that's independent of the person, something that can be donned and doffed like a suit of clothes.

Our research and that of our colleagues has shown that, far from being a superficial form of communication that can be consciously manipulated, nonverbal-communication systems are interwoven into the fabric of the personality and, as sociologist Erving Goffman has demonstrated, into society itself. They are the warp and woof of daily interaction with others and they influence how one expresses oneself, how one experiences oneself as a man or a woman.

Nonverbal communications signal to members of your own group what kind of person you are, how you feel about others, how you'll fit into and work in a group, whether you're assured or anxious, the degree to which you feel comfortable with the standards of your own culture, as well as deeply significant feelings about the self, including the state of your own psyche. For most of us, it's difficult to accept the reality of another's behavioral system. And, of course, none of us will ever become fully knowledgeable of the importance of every nonverbal signal. But as long as each of us realizes the power of these signals, this society's diversity can be a source of great strength rather than a further —and subtly powerful—source of division.

Be careful, now.

Don't take the generalizations you've just read and plant them in your mind as Truth. The observations made by the Halls are not the last word on any aspect of body language, as they would admit. Every statement is subject to challenge.

For example, remember the comment that body functions such as eye pupillary reflex are beyond a person's control? Well, a great deal of research is now underway that already suggests that the so-called involuntary body functions are subject to deliberate self-control. Scientists have developed biofeedback equipment that helps people alter their body temperature, heart rate, and brain waves. Yogis from the East have been teaching this for many hundreds of years, but we in the West more readily believe our gauges and gadgets—which are now confirming much suggested by the ancients.

Another example, the distance zones of "intimate, personal, social, and public" proposed in the article. Ed Hall's initial sample, from whom the conclusions were drawn, included only a few hundred people. And they were all eastern seaboard, professional and semi-professional persons. Is it prudent for us to conclude that "*most* white middle-class Americans" experience these zones? Maybe not.

Make your own observations, I say.

Verify through *your* experience.

In these early days of research on nonverbal behavior, almost anyone can become an "expert" rather quickly. So little has been done yet. And as is often true in newly emerging fields of study, true experts turn up in the most unexpected places.

I have learned much about nonverbal body language from bartenders. Policemen. Prostitutes. Actors. Salesmen. Tailors. Dancers. Psychiatrists. My grandmother. My children. Even family pets, who are amazingly accurate in their observations and responses to body cues.

WHO MIGHT TEACH YOU SOMETHING OF BODY TALK?

Some of the questions that are kicking around in my head, and that still need answering, might be helpful to you in focusing your thoughts about this area of nonverbal communication. I want to share them with you.

NUTRITION

1. Is my body color (eyes, flesh, nails, teeth) related to my diet?
2. Is my skin condition (wrinkles, dryness, softness, healing and/or scarring) influenced by my diet?
3. Is my muscle movement pattern (tonus and coordination) affected by my diet?
4. Are my bodily smells in any way connected to my diet?

1. Do human beings have a biological *need* to be touched? Or is touch behavior simply culturally learned?
2. What are my culture's touch rules between people of opposite sex, age differences, status differences, race differences?
3. Are human touch patterns related to body energy fields, as suggested by Kirlian photography, acupuncture, and measurable electromagnetic energy generated by the human body?
4. What are the "do's and don'ts" of my daily touching behavior?
5. Does "visual touching" (exposed skin areas) mean permission for contact touching?

SMELL

1. Do humans react to body smells as other animals do?
2. Can I recognize another person by his own unique body smell, house smell, clothing smell?
3. Is human body smell affected by emotional changes?
4. How have the cosmetic, perfume, and deodorant industries influenced my world of smell?

POSTURE

1. What are *reliable* body cues to tension versus relaxation?
2. Is there any connection between outward posture and internal emotional state?
3. What is the role of balance in posture cues?

FACINGNESS/FRONTALITY

1. What is communicated when people turn away from one another (in varying degrees)?
2. What is communicated when people directly face one another with face, shoulders, hips, and legs?

3. What, if any, are the differences in the facingness behavior of opposite-sexed people, persons of various age levels, and people of separate classes or status positions?

FACIAL DISPLAY

1. What is the importance of the face, in comparison with the other parts of the body, in nonverbal communication?
2. What eye behaviors do I use in my daily interactions?
3. With my vision eliminated, how does my perception of other people change?

CLOTHING/COSMETIC

1. What are the known cultural rules on *hair* display (head, face, legs and arms) relating to sex role, age level, status?
2. How does skin display relate to clothing messages?
3. How are the rules of clothing cues established and enforced? How extinguished?

My reason for being interested in such questions is that this kind of body language gives my words a backup system. Often my body signals convey what I mean even when my words fail, when people don't understand my conversation. And that's important to me.

Of course, such physical language of the body is only *one* vocabulary. Only one part of a much larger picture. Nonverbal communication expresses life energy on many levels, through many modes.

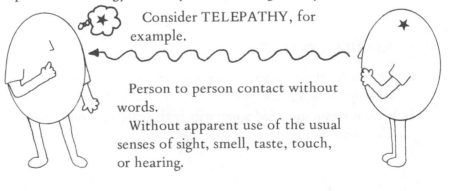

Consider TELEPATHY, for example.

Person to person contact without words.

Without apparent use of the usual senses of sight, smell, taste, touch, or hearing.

Telepathy is a phenomenon well established by responsible research in many countries, although people who haven't investigated the rigorous studies conducted frequently think of mind-to-mind contact as nonsense, carnival, hocus-pocus.

For my part, I *know* telepathy functions because I experience it in my daily life. By that I mean that my wife and I often carry on conversations in which only part of the words heard are actually spoken. A very simple example occurred last week while I was getting ready for work, and was standing at the bathroom sink, shaving. Paula (my wife) was in the kitchen, and I heard her ask me about some legal papers. I answered her question, and in a few seconds she appeared in the bathroom door with that look on her face that said, "You did it again." She had been thinking about the legal matter, but had not said a thing about it all morning. Nor had she spoken to me when I "heard" her question.

WHAT EXPERIENCES HAVE
YOU HAD WITH TELEPATHY?

A friend of mine who is a milkman uses telepathy in his work and family life. For instance, when his wife needs to contact him during the day she simply "tunes him in" (his words) and he locates a telephone wherever he happens to be and calls her for specifics. They haven't the ability to transmit grocery lists, because they've tried, but they can send back and forth simple distress signals. It's not a coincidence, either, because he does not make phone calls to her as a matter of routine or habit.

To many people, I realize, such stories seem incredible or, at best, unscientific. Yes, these anecdotal examples are unscientific. That's why I would urge such people to look into the truly valid scientific efforts to explore the nonverbal mode of telepathy.

It is curious that most folks I talk with think of telepathy only between people. But if it can happen between human beings, then isn't it possible that it occurs between other life forms? Perhaps even between humans and other living creatures?

In pursuit of that question, I invite you to read of the work of Mr. Cleve Backster and his lie-detectored household plants. He cannot be classified as a radical or carnival huckster, but the implications of his work suggest a fascinating mode of nonverbal communication.

Startling New Research from the Man Who "Talks" to Plants

BY JANICE AND CHARLES ROBBINS

You may recall the name Cleve Backster. It belongs to the man who attached a lie-detector to the leaf of a plant and got the surprise of his life. The plant showed reactions similar to those of a human being. In subsequent experiments, Backster discovered that plants are hooked into some kind of telepathic communication system and that they are highly sensitized to people, to the destruction of animal life and to threats to their own well-being.

National Wildlife published the first account of Mr. Backster's findings (February-March 1969, pages 4-8), and the article attracted worldwide attention. Secretaries and housewives began talking to their plants and treating them with tender loving care. Comedians made the expected jokes; *Dracaena massangeana* and philodendron became household words.

That is history now. To get caught up on what has been happening to Mr. Backster lately, we called on him again.

He is to be found in a suite of small rooms—crowded with scientific apparatus and plants—in an ordinary office building just off Times Square in New York. Here he pursues his vocation, which is teaching the technique of the lie-detector, or polygraph, to policemen and other interested parties . . . and his avocation, which is pure research into the secrets of nature.

We were ushered into a miniature room containing a metal desk with a polygraph countersunk in its top and several plants of the hotel-lobby variety. In his shirtsleeves, Backster sat at the desk, if "sit" is the word for someone who radiates energy and seems to be in constant motion. Now 47, he looks 10 years younger, has the body of an athlete and a disarming friendliness.

What had been happening? Well, quite a lot. He's been making speeches at universities, at Yale to an audience of linguists on nonverbal communication, at MIT on plant sensitivity, at Dartmouth to biologists and at North Carolina to botanists.

Between 25 and 30 universities are supposed to be "replicating"—duplicating—his major experiment, an extremely sophisticated one involving plants and brine shrimp. So far the results have not been published, but more than 7,000 scientists all over the world have written in for reports of his original research.

A foundation has expressed interest in subsidizing him. He has appeared in numerous radio and TV shows. And, most important, he has embarked on two more experiments that complement and expand his earlier work.

It took a little persuading to get him to talk about them since they are still "in progress." But we succeeded.

The first experiment is an effort to condition reflexes in plants much as the famous Russian scientist Pavlov did in dogs. Pavlov would ring a bell each time a dog ate; finally the mere ringing of the bell, without the food, would cause the dog to salivate. Any such effect, of course, depends on memory, and various observations have convinced Backster that his plants possess the equivalent of memory.

Plant memory of a sort was suggested in one of Backster's early experiments, in which six of his polygraph students participated. One was chosen by lot to destroy a plant. Keeping his identity from Backster, the criminal committed his deed secretly, with only another plant as witness. Then Backster hooked a polygraph up to the surviving plant, and the six subjects paraded into the room in turns. Five of them caused no noticeable reaction in the witness plant, but the sixth, the killer, sent it into a tizzy.

As Backster is careful to point out, the plant could have been reflecting the guilt feelings of the culprit. Still, there's an even chance that it was *remembering* him, since the man was not exactly overwhelmed with guilt.

At any rate, to settle the memory question, Backster has begun applying Pavlovian methods to plants. He has rigged up some electrified trolley wires, which run down the hall and turn into the room where the plant of the experiment is stationed. Six small, identical cups—one holding seeds, another worms, a third insects, etc.—are attached to the trolley and circulate at intervals. One of the six is the object to which Backster wants to condition the plant, and he uses light as the stimulus.

For this purpose, he connected a light-conducting electrode to both the polygraph and the plant, bathing the latter with light each time the conditioning cup reaches it. Will the plant in time learn to pick out that one cup from among the six and react without the light? Backster thinks so, but his hopes will not be allowed to compromise the flawlessly automated experiment.

EGGS WITH FEELINGS. His second experiment concerns eggs—chicken eggs. He once had a dog, which used to hang around the laboratory, and each night he would feed it a raw egg. Soon he noticed that the plants connected to the polygraph in a nearby room were reacting strenuously to the breaking of the egg. Then one night, wondering how the egg itself might be feeling, Backster attached his polygraph electrodes to *that.*

He got a nine-hour recording, part of which showed pulsations: the heartbeat of a chick embryo. By means of the egg carton, Backster checked back on the origin of the egg and learned that it had undoubtedly been fertilized (most store-bought eggs are not). The recorded heartbeat was accurate for the embryo. But when he dissected the egg, he was astonished to find that it contained no physical, circulatory structure to account for the pulsation.

"So," he asks, "what was I into? Was this some kind of entree into the origin-of-life sort of thing?"

What he's into now is a series of egg experiments involving the interplay between plants and eggs, as well as eggs and eggs (shake one and you get a reaction in another). He's trying to find out if eggs from the same hen react to each other in the same way as those from different hens, and so on.

Plants, he's found, don't react much to each other; their attunement is mostly to animal life, especially human life. Eggs on the other hand are mutually sensitive. He has already found that the destruction of an egg at one end of the laboratory will predictably cause great agitation in a second egg at the other end.

"When the egg knows you're going

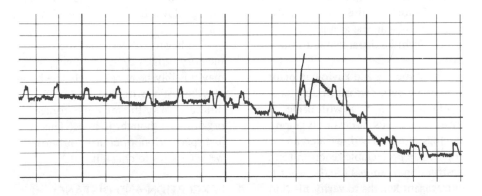

A nine-hour recording obtained by attaching polygraph electrodes to an egg turned up the heartbeat of a chick embryo. The egg had indeed been fertilized, but dissection revealed no physical, circulatory structure to account for the pulsation.

122 to break it or cook it," we asked, "does it react the same way the plant does?"

"Yes, it goes into a state of shock," he replied. "It faints. Plants do the same thing—and vegetables. Higher forms of animal life don't seem to get the point so quickly. The rabbi's

prayer before the slaughtering of animals for kosher food gives notice of intent to kill and allows the animals to go into a configuration, which is like a state of shock. So the violence doesn't leave a residue in the animal cells which might be disagreeable to the taste."

Both the egg and Pavlovian plant studies are outgrowths of Backster's celebrated experiment with brine shrimp. After his earliest polygraph tracings of plants had revealed an apparently predictable reaction to the destruction of animal life, he went to extravagant lengths to verify his findings.

His subjects were three different plants, each closeted in its own room and separately attached to a poly-graph. At the other end of the office was an apparatus of his invention which at random intervals dumped bowlsful of brine shrimp into simmering water. The experiment took place late at night, with no human being around, and the results were always the same. Each time the shrimp hit the boiling water the plants—separately, at the same moment, behind doors—registered an emotional reaction on the polygraph.

The implications of this experiment and of the two Backster now has underway are—well, staggering. And they don't stop with plants and eggs.

"We've also been working with cell cultures," he says, "and with amoeba, paramecium, fresh fruits and vegetables, mold cultures and blood samples. We find they all appear to have the same capability as plants. What I call 'primary perception.' Our experiments imply that total memory may go down to single-cell level, at least.

"It begins to seem that the memory capability—even in people—may possibly be at cell level. The brain may be just a switching mechanism, not necessarily the memory storage organ we've thought it to be. This is just speculation, of course, but now we have ways to check it out."

PERCEPTION AND DISTANCE.
Another thing Backster would like to check out is the relationship, if any, between primary perception and distance.

"I'm trying to get the space people to do something with a Mars probe," he says, "to show that distance doesn't limit primary perception."

He'd like to put (1) a plant, complete with polygraph, on a Mars probe and (2) the person attuned to it, the one who cares for it, in Ground Control, Houston. Then he would expose the person to a programmed electric or emotional shock and have the plant's reaction telemetered back to earth.

"Ordinarily it takes a telemetered signal 6 to 6½ minutes to get to Mars and 6 to 6½ minutes back. The question would be how quickly we would receive the plant's reaction to the person's stimulus. If it comes back in 6 minutes, how did it get out there? Even if it takes 12 minutes, overall, it would be great to know that that enormous distance is no barrier to primary perception.

MAY NOT USE TIME. "But I suspect that this signal would return in half the time. If it did, you'd have proof that there is a non-time-consuming form of communication, a phenomenon entirely beside or outside the electromagnetic spectrum."

He added, "We keep hearing about non-time-consuming communication from Eastern religious sources. They tell us that the universe is in balance; if it happens to go out of balance someplace, you can't wait a hundred light-years for the imbalance to be discovered and corrected. This non-time-consuming communication, this

oneness among all living things, would be the answer."

National Wildlife: *Going back to your laboratory experiments, do you feel that the attunement between a person and a plant is the same as between two people?*

Cleve Backster: I'm sure of it. But it's nothing we can explain in the context of our present scientific knowledge.

NW: *Don't you think it's easier between people?*

CB: No. People are too complicated. Plants are the ones that excel at this. We should take our lessons from plants; they're simpler, more direct.

NW: *Does this have any effect on the plant itself—when it receives a strong emotion from someone else, for instance?*

CB: It changes the electrical potential discharge of the plant—this is what we're picking up. If we continually think derogatory thoughts about a plant, for example, or talk about it in a derogatory way, and if we praise another plant, we can get the first plant to do poorly, or even die, and the other to grow by leaps and bounds. This has been done by high school fair students all over the country. I've got a whole rash of correspondence from them.

NW: *What about poison plants everybody hates? They must have a terrible time.*

124   CB: (laughing) It's like crab grass.
      There are some plants that just
      won't listen.

NW: *But in your research now you're
moving more into the egg and the
animal, aren't you?*

CB: Well, I don't want to go too high,
not really to the animal level because
there are too many committed people there. People haven't committed
themselves on plants. The botanists
don't debate the levels of consciousness in plants because they haven't
conceded any consciousness. When
you get up to the egg level no one
has committed himself about consciousness there, either. I know
where to stop. I'm not interfering
with committed people, so they're
showing me nothing but pure interest—they're not on the defensive.

*Whether he is experimenting with plants, or
recording the heartbeat of chick embryos,
lie-detector expert Cleve Backster knows he
faces the same kind of criticism that has
always greeted those who throw science a
"curve."*

It falls to few men to throw
science a real curve, as Cleve Backster
at this writing appears to have done.
Newton did it with an apple, Darwin
with an ape, the Wright brothers, a
flying machine. All of them risked
ridicule, ostracism, or worse.

Backster is well aware of the
hazards he faces; they're one of the
reasons he leans over backward in his
experiments to follow scientific
methodology to the letter. And in his
relations with various groups,
especially organized science, he has
charted his course with the same care.

"I use a very low-key approach
with scientists," he explains. " 'Gee

whiz,' I say, 'look what happens when
I hook electrodes to a plant. Can you
help me?' And before they're through,
they're hooked."

While we had been talking,
Backster had attached a couple of
electrodes to a leaf of the philodendron in the corner of his office, then
turned on the desk-top polygraph.
Slowly the chart unreeled; the single
pen moved eerily back and forth,
recording the plant's electrical
impulses. A few minutes later, while
he was out of the room, two men

came to the door, asking for him, and the plant greeted them with some emotion. It turned out they were police officers who dropped in to get caught up on their lie-detector homework.

Their arrival prompted us to ask Backster when he returned if plants had ever been used to participate in a real criminal investigation. He said they had, once, in a murder case.

PLANTS WITNESSED MURDER. "A girl was murdered in a large factory, and I was retained by the police to give lie detector tests to the prime suspects," he said. "A huge maintenance crew had been there on the evening the girl was working overtime. One of them could possibly have been in a position to commit the crime. Ordinary interrogation procedures presented a problem, because of the large number of suspects. As there were a couple of plants in the office where the body had been found, I suggested that we attach polygraph electrodes to them, and ask each of

the workers into an adjoining office, one at a time. If the plants did their thing, the whole business might be expedited.

"The plants," he explained, "didn't spot the murderer, as the apparent solution to the crime did not involve a company employee." He added, with a smile, "It was interesting to note the reaction of the seasoned law enforcement officers, when I requested that they place the plants in a locked room each night to provide protective custody to the sole witnesses of the homicide."

DO YOU KNOW ANYONE WITH A "GREEN THUMB"? WHAT KIND OF ATTITUDE DOES THAT PERSON HAVE TOWARD PLANT LIFE?

I've noticed that people who love plants seem to have much better "luck" growing them than those who are indifferent. Is that true in your experience? If so, how do you account for that difference?

Although I do not have the electronic equipment to duplicate Backster's work, I have tried something which seems related and which you, too, might enjoy.

I have deliberately raised one plant with love, and one plant with indifference. Came from the same seed, planted in same soil (but separate pots), exposed to same sun/shade, same temperature and humidity, same nutrients. The only difference in their rearing was that one of them I took out three times a day for ten-minute "love sessions" in which I silently expressed concern for its health and well-being. I visualized it growing luxuriantly, full bodied and flowered; talked to it about proper use of its nutrients. And at bed time, I said good-night to it.

The other plant received the same physical environment, but no thoughts for its welfare. No individual attention. No companionship, literally.

As measured against a ruler, the plant for which I had held loving thoughts grew taller, wider, faster, and had more blossoms than the "unloved" plant.

And I have repeated this experiment with mung beans, peas, sweet peas, and marigolds. Once I was surprised because the unloved plant caught up with the loved plant in size, after an initial difference that was noticeable. But upon questioning my entire family, it turned out that my brother Larry had been mistakenly flourishing his attention on the wrong plant! And Larry has strong vibes.

While this simple growing experiment does not prove anything about telepathy between plants and people, it is at least suggestive.

WHY DON'T YOU TRY IT, AND FIND OUT FOR YOURSELF?

Of course, everything presented so far in this chapter has concerned immediate, here-and-now communication. Face-to-face or mind-to-mind.

But there are other modes of nonverbal cues that are important and express themselves through a more extended time frame. Men communicate with men through time.

I speak here of the use of inanimate symbols that truly affect our daily behavior. Some authorities make a distinction between symbols and "signals," but I consider that an academic difference, not one that is real in daily living.

Author David Dempsey offers some insight into this other realm of nonverbal cues, with such baiting statements as:

> *A change in the color of our surroundings changes the pattern of human movement.*

> *Whether space is friendly or alien often depends upon size and layout.*

> *Noise is an environmental variable which profoundly affects our moods, our performance at work and even our dream life.*

As you read this article, consider the nonverbal symbols/signals in the environment of your place of work, or your home, school, or community. See if you can "read" the cues of which Dempsey writes here.

Man's Hidden Environment

Ever since Adam and Eve were banished from the Garden of Eden, man has known that his surroundings influence his behavior. The houses we live in, our offices, the space around us, the sounds that intrude on our daily lives, smells, colors, even the arrangement of furniture, determine many of our actions. A well-known contemporary architect, for example, claimed that he could design a house that would guarantee a divorce for any couple who lived in it a month.

Man obviously has evolved along with his environment, modifying it to suit his needs. But somewhere along the line, the process got out of hand; the technical side of modern civilization assumed a life of its own that no longer reflected the true needs of its users. Technology, in conquering nature, has surrounded us with a unique man-made environment, but for most of us, our physical comforts have made us ill at ease psychologi-

cally. And our psychological landscape has a profound effect on how we behave. For example:

The decor of a room can influence the speed at which we work. In an experiment at Brandeis University, lab assistants were assigned three rooms— "ugly," "beautiful," and "average"— for the purpose of giving tests. Examiners in the ugly room almost always finished their testing faster than those in the two other rooms. Moral: Beauty in the environment may not be a virtue if there is work to be done.

A change in the color of our surroundings changes the pattern of human movement. At the University of Kansas' art museum, investigators tested the effects of different colored walls on two groups of visitors to an exhibition of prints. For the first group, the room was painted light beige; for the second, dark brown. Movement was traced by a switch mat under the carpet that electrically mapped the visitors' footsteps. It was found that those who entered the dark room walked more quickly, covered more area and spent less time in the room than the people in the beige environment. For whatever reason, dark brown stimulated more activity, but the activity was concluded sooner.

Noise is an environmental variable that we take for granted, yet it profoundly affects our moods, our performance at work and even our dream life. One psychiatrist testified before a New York State legislative committee that the interruption of nighttime dreams by the jet rush of planes impaired the mental health of those who lived near Kennedy Airport. Dreams, he said, were broken off before they could unblock the repressions that were bottled up in the unconscious.

Until recently, it was assumed that sheer loudness was the culprit in noisy situations, but psychologists have concluded that unevenness of sound is more damaging. A factory going full blast on a programmed schedule was judged quieter than a bank whose machines operated in fits and starts; the bank finally had to hire deaf people to reduce employee turnover.

At Columbia University, in an investigation of the effect of density on behavior, it was found that people working in an extremely crowded room performed just as efficiently as people who were not crowded. However, men under crowded condi-

tions became competitive, suspicious and combative; whereas women were *less* competitive, more intimate and easier to get along with. In a follow-up experiment, the groups listened to taped courtroom cases and were asked to render verdicts of guilt or innocence. Results showed that men in a smaller, crowded room handed out more severe punishment than those who deliberated in a spacious environment. The women's verdicts, however, were not appreciably affected by the size or crowding of the room.

Sociologist-architect Kyoshi Izumi, at the University of Saskatchewan at Regina, says that the use of plastics to simulate wood, metal, leather, cloth— even plants—sets up an element of doubt in our sensing mechanism that is inconsistent with what we instinctively feel the environment ought to be. Subconsciously, we resist the synthetic world as we grope for the natural.

The sheer size of many buildings we live and work in and the sterility of much of the "overdesigned" modern architecture are defeating, too, because they make it difficult for us to involve ourselves with such super-structures in any meaningful way. This has been cited as the reason for the sabotage of Eero Saarinen's stunning but sterile CBS Building in New York by employees who cluttered and even defaced their offices in an effort to personalize their working space.

Monotony of decor, the endless corridors of large buildings, the rows of desks in an office suggest that we are on a treadmill and, in Izumi's words, adversely affect "comfortably perceived psychic time." For most

people, Izumi thinks, time is measured visually; when there is an absence of clues, our sense of continuity is diminished and we "lose track of time."

Another theory holds that such "timeless" environments can make us anxious because we are unable to see a future—and that our environment must provide not only a future but a past and a present as well. Using hypnosis, Dr. Bernard Aaronson was able to induce various combinations of this time sense in a group of subjects and, in so doing, create abnormal states of mind. Suggesting no past, but only a future, brought on a manic condition. When no future was suggested, there was depression. The rapid build-up of gleaming, glass-walled schools and office buildings is believed by many psychologists to partly explain the existential anxiety so pervasive in the industrial nations. Such ultra-modern structures cut us off from the familiar, human milieu of our childhood. This appears to be particularly true of buildings that depart from square or rectangular form. In his study of the radically designed French Radio and Television headquarters in Paris, psychiatrist Paul Sivadon found an abnormal degree of depression among the personnel. One reason for this, he concluded, was that the long circular corridors, by blocking orientation with the outside environ-ment, create feelings of insecurity. A lack of intersecting corridors also contributes to the sense of being trapped; people don't know where they are at any given moment.

Until the early 1960s, most of what we knew about human responses to outside stimuli came from laboratory experiments or was extrapolated from the behavior of animals. Ivan Pavlov's famous conditioned-reflex theory was based on his work with dogs. By ringing a bell during feeding periods, the Russian scientist conditioned his animals to salivate when the bell was rung, even if there was no food. George Bernard Shaw, when told of this experiment, remarked, "If they had brought me this problem, I could have given them the same answer without torturing a single dog."

Moreover, the environment we observe is not necessarily the "real" environment; depending on our personality, our ethnic background or simply our mood, what we perceive may be a distortion of what actually exists. In Los Angeles, when asked to map the city from memory, students at UCLA saw it as a whole. For the black residents of Watts, however, the important landmarks were the county hospital and the city jail, where so many of them had been taken after the riots. In the jargon of sociology, their perception of the city was culturally biased.

All of us at some time look at the environment through the distorting

131

> *The environment serves as a "magnetic field" of subtle and wide-ranging psychological forces that we modify by the way we interact with it.*

The shortcoming of the behaviorist approach—whose most persuasive spokesman today is Harvard educator B. F. Skinner—is its extremely narrow view of man's relationship to his physical environment. For most of us, it's not so much the carrot and the stick that influence our actions (although they may play a part) but the constantly shifting physical and social surroundings in which we live and work. In a sense, the environment serves as a "magnetic field" of subtle and wide-ranging psychological forces that we, in turn, modify by the way we interact with it.

lenses of anger, annoyance and frustration. At Ohio State University, students were asked to estimate the distance from the campus to various points in Columbus. Surprisingly, newcomers were remarkably accurate, but students familiar with the city greatly overestimated the number of miles to the central business section. Impatience with traffic lights and stop signs, and the frayed nerves from downtown driving, had made the distance seem farther than it was.

We know that the prick of a needle in our hand brings an immediate reflex—a withdrawal from pain. A

132 blinding flash of light will make us close our eyes. These are simple, protective responses to "unfriendly" stimuli. But we are only beginning to learn how people adapt to less obvious changes. At the Graduate Center of the City University of New York, psychologists have created an ingenious "perception" room to discover how people act in a physical setting with which they have had no previous experience. It includes a welter of sights and sounds that have no obvious relationship to one another, yet all of which compete for attention.

As a volunteer subject, I found myself in a dim 18′ X 26′ room surrounded by aluminized mirrors that vibrated at various frequencies as I approached them.

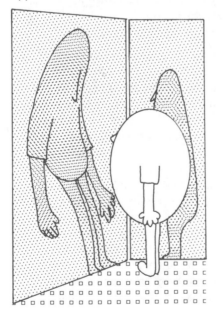

Gargoylelike reflections were thrown back at me; strobe lights flashed weirdly at my feet; the mirrors gave off a low, rumbling sound and pictures were cast onto walls from overhead slide projectors. The entire ensemble was programmed and driven by a central console in an adjacent room, and my reactions—startled movements, sustained interests, avoidance, random explorations—were recorded on a cylinder-and-pen device similar to an electrocardiograph. Essentially, this instrument traced two things: (1) how long I remained in front of a given mirror, with its accompanying bombardment of lights, sounds, and images; and (2) whether my response to this contradictory information—moving closer, shielding my eyes, deactivating the sound by moving farther away, etc.—favored one means of perception over another.

The psychologists at City University are still cautious about their findings, but here are some promising theories: When we are subjected to several competing stimuli, we tend to convert them into a single sensory message. In short, we translate the information into our strongest suit. Artists and other visually minded people "see" sound and describe it in terms of light and color; musicians "hear" paintings and strobe lights and sense a rhythmic, even a melodic, pattern in them. The experiments suggest that people who can perceive their surroundings by thus translating from one sense to another maintain a longer interest in the environment and find more meaning in it.

What are the practical values of all these theories? Urban planners are learning that if man is to be psychologically comfortable, he must be able to make sense out of the clutter of city life. Knowing in advance how we respond to sounds, lights, open spaces, the varieties of buildings and street layouts—what our behavioral expectations of the urban environment are— helps us create the kinds of neighborhoods we want. In some instances, planners use play money in a Monopolylike game to determine what it is that residents of a community value most about their physical environment. In Boston, designer Michael Southworth blindfolds his subjects and has them pushed around in wheelchairs while they dictate their reactions and feelings of "sonic distress" and "sonic delight" for the guidance of planners who seek to reduce unwanted sound.

In most cases, however, the new psychodesign is empirical. San Francisco architect Piero N. Patri moves into his housing developments for a month or so to test their livability. He keeps an anthropologist on his staff because he is convinced that ethnic culture influences housing preferences. Recently, before starting a low-income urban-renewal project, Patri organized an encounter group in which prospective tenants (mostly black) confronted architects and designers (all white) in a marathon

session that sought to uncover the life style of those who would occupy the buildings. The session brought out the bottled-up hostility of the prospective tenants: "Don't give us another high-rise slum," they said, in effect. "We deserve better." Result: an attractive development of three-story, individually designed town houses that are a radical departure from the ghetto. Patri believes that many large housing projects are turned into slums because tenants lack a sense of "turf." Like their middle-class counterparts in the new office buildings, they mess up such developments in an attempt to assert their individuality.

The mentally ill are especially sensitive to their surroundings, and much of what we've learned about the designed environment has been discovered in the psychiatric ward. Several years ago, Izumi was hired to plan a psychiatric center in Yorkton, Saskatchewan. Among his impressions: The ward's physical environment created too much ambiguity in the minds of the patients. Free-hanging clocks seemed to defy gravity; transoms suggested guillotines about to fall; polished-terazzo surfaces and uniformity of design confused the patients' sense of time and space.

Izumi's plans for Yorkton were finally scaled to the psychic boundaries of the patients and design was used to reinforce a feeling of security and intimacy in a complex of several small, rectangular buildings. All the structural elements were familiar,

134 Izumi stressed, and there were no illusory qualities of the kinds that architects so often try to achieve in striving to make things seem what they aren't. He would immunize ambiguity in the environment even for healthy people, since, in his opinion, all of us tense up in the face of uncertainty.

Another behavioral scientist, Dr. Humphry Osmond, contrasts "sociopetal" space—that which draws people together—with "sociofugal" space, which pushes them apart. A New England common is sociopetal; a row of glassed-in cubicles is usually sociofugal. If you want privacy, you seek out the latter, but not all common areas are necessarily socializing. One of the puzzles that confronted a team of psychologists was why patients in multibed rooms were more passive in their behavior than those in small rooms. In mapping patient activity, the team found that in the larger rooms, occupants spent from two-thirds to three-fourths of their time lying on their beds, either asleep or awake. But in smaller two-bed rooms, patients were socially interactive. It was concluded that what really matters is the freedom of choice permitted the patient in what he does; the more people in a room the less chance each has to pursue his own activities. Without choice, one tends to withdraw.

Observations in the outside world also confirm this. A comparison of large and small schools showed that although there were more opportuni-

ties for varied activities in the bigger institutions, there was more individual participation in the smaller ones. Ideal space may be that which permits us to maintain our privacy while interacting with others, for we are social in small groups. Robert Sommer, a psychologist at the University of California at Davis, believes there is a spatial behavior that influences many of our actions. He observed that in restaurants, people are more likely to talk

across the corner of a table than if sitting opposite or side by side. The shape of the table also makes a difference. Those with straight sides help define our boundaries and make us more confident and assertive. Round tables seem to promote equality and uncertainty. Men will seldom sit side by side if they are given a chance to sit opposite, but women prefer sitting next to each other.

Additionally, in a study of the seating arrangements of school children in 4000 classrooms, it was found that half the pupils with chronic infections and two-thirds of those with nutritional problems occupied seats in the darkest quadrant of the rooms. Sommer suggests that social disadvantage and physical impairment probably led these children to select— or be assigned to—inferior space. In all behavior, there is a strong desire to stake out a turf that's appropriate to our self-image. Moreover, the milieu helps dictate the role we play in it. That we act like students when we are in school, are reverential in church and lackadaisical in parks is because these environments tell us in advance how to behave.

In all behavior, there is a strong desire to stake out a turf that's appropriate to our self-image.

A revealing example of this occurred when the Napa State Hospital in California was heavily damaged by the earthquake of 1906. To the surprise of the authorities, when the psychiatric patients were moved into tents and were no longer walled in, their behavior and cooperation improved measurably. Epileptics undergoing treatment experienced fewer fits and, in general, the tent colony seemed to benefit everyone,

even the staff. But when the buildings were restored, behavior returned to normal—patients became difficult and the epileptics had more fits. Psychiatrists concluded that in any environment, there are standards of behavior to which people adhere simply because it's what's expected of them.

Whether space is friendly or alien often depends upon size and layout. Parks, for example, bring people together on a casual basis, but they also promote distancing for those who want to be alone, and they are ideal for lovers who seek a public setting in which to advertise their private feelings. Formal gardens, on the other hand, impose formal conduct; the landscaping discourages social interaction. Contrary to what one might expect, private outdoor space is more socializing than communal space. Residents of a postwar housing development near Coventry, England, fraternized more with their neighbors when they met in each other's yards; families that were compelled to share a common garden actually knew fewer neighbors. In suburbs and small towns, people are more likely to talk across their back yards if the property line is indicated by a fence. Because this boundary helps them maintain territoriality, it actually brings neighbors closer together.

If both privacy and social interaction are necessary ingredients of human behavior, how do we arrange our territory to gain the optimum values of each? Environmentalists see

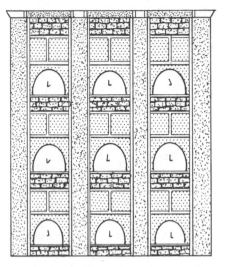

this as a problem in spatial separation, and they've had a field day working out the answers. Here are some of their findings:

In a study made in Topeka, Kansas, the Environmental Research and Development Foundation compared the effects of high-rise and garden apartments on the behavior of their occupants. Results showed that, proportionately, the low-rise tenants made twice as many friends inside their building area as did the high-rise tenants. Moreover, in the taller structures, people exhibited greater feelings of indifference and withdrawal, while garden apartment dwellers were more involved in politics, civic life, etc., and enjoyed a greater sense of power over their lives.

A study in Germany compared the health of wives and children of British soldiers living in separate houses with the health of those in apartment buildings. The differences were startling. Among the latter group, the illness rate was 57 percent higher, with neuroses showing a markedly greater incidence. And within the apartment buildings, the *rates* of neuroses varied directly with the distance from the ground floor: Higher apartments seemingly created more social isolation. In short, the effect of mass housing is not crowding but loneliness.

In explaining this paradox, architect Christopher Alexander of the Center for Environmental Structure in Berkeley, California, posits another: It isn't stress itself that causes the ills of urban life, he says, but the turning away from it. "Stress forces people to withdraw into themselves (and) creates more people who believe in self-sufficiency as an ideal, making intimate contact seem less necessary." Alexander would "bring people out of hiding" through an ingenious geometric city of transparent houses, open courtyards and private connecting spaces, all buried just below the surface of the earth in clusters of 28 buildings. In a sense, he would bury people to encourage intimacy.

Reminiscent of a Pueblo cliff dweller's setup, Alexander's utopia has yet to be constructed, but the theory of forced contact may not be as crazy as it seems. Robert K. Merton analyzed families who lived on opposite sides of a street. He found that 75 percent of the people who had doors facing the front made contact with their across-the-street neighbors. Of those who didn't, only four percent became friends.

Crowding as an environmental variable is only beginning to be seriously examined, and the data so far is inconclusive. Much of what we know about the subject on a hypothetical level can be traced to Dr. John B. Calhoun's experiments with Norwegian rats. Calhoun, who is a research psychologist at the National Institute of Mental Health, demonstrated that when rats in confinement exceed a certain density, they undergo radical changes in behavior. Some become homosexual; others become aggressive; yet others simply lie down and die. Many ecologists have concluded from this that there is an upper limit to man's own tolerance for crowding, quite apart from his demands on the natural resources. Calhoun believes that, based on the total ecological picture, the optimum world population is nine billion, but he sees little hope that the increase can be stopped before it reaches 13.5 billion.

This need not be fatal, however. There is a good chance that many of the adverse effects noted in the crowding experiments—the combative behavior of men, the morbid effects on animals—are really the result of confinement. When people are free to escape—via the automobile, for instance—high density is more tolerable. And whether we *feel* crowded often depends upon the social setting. At a cocktail party, people bunch up

intentionally to get in on the action. But a golf course is crowded if a foursome 200 yards away is holding up the play. The important thing is not how many people live on an acre of land but how they arrange themselves on it and for what purpose.

There does seem to be a relationship between spatial separation and our proneness to antisocial behavior. A study made in France found a direct correlation between living space, crime and other social problems among the urban working class. The optimum turf proved to be from 85 to 130 square feet per person. When space was less than 85, social pathology doubled. Above 130 square feet, the disorders also increased, although not so drastically.

If high density is a factor in crime and disease, Hong Kong should be a prime example. It is the most densely populated city in the world, containing up to 2000 people per acre (compared with 450 in Boston and New York). As many as four or five

families occupy the same apartment on a shift basis. Yet, except for tuberculosis, its inhabitants appear to be healthier than Americans, and far more law-abiding. A survey based on census figures for 1961 showed 9.3 deaths per 1000 population in the United States and 5.9 in Hong Kong. Fewer than one tenth as many Hong Kong residents were hospitalized for psychiatric disorders as in the U.S. (partly, no doubt, because of fewer diagnostic and treatment facilities, although the discrepancy is nevertheless startling). Our figures for murder and manslaughter were six times as high and that for all serious crimes combined was double. Yet when new housing was made available to some Hong Kong families, many of them sublet space in their tiny apartments to others.

Why these disparities exist isn't entirely clear, but we can speculate that abundant public-health care and the highly organized Chinese family help keep a damper on the runaway problems of urban life. Orientals, too, have a higher involvement ratio than do most white Americans (so, for that matter, do southern Europeans and American blacks); hence they survive comfortably in environments that we consider intolerable. The Japanese have adapted to high densities by leaving their cities chaotic and unplanned while beautifying the interiors of their homes.

One of the dilemmas encountered by urban planners in this country is why uprooted slum dwellers often move to another slum rather than into new housing projects elsewhere in the city. Studies have shown that many of these ethnic groups are quite happy to be crowded. Professor Izumi thinks that ghettos are environmentally permissive in that they offer a freer range of choice. In the planned community of Brasilia, the new capital of Brazil, it is the older, "free city" of the working classes to which other residents flee to experience spontaneity and excitement—the same reason that suburban New Yorkers flock to Manhattan.

The new towns of Europe, with their unified design and careful landscaping, apparently induce a degree of apathy in their inhabitants that is not experienced in the urban "jungle." Last year, a team of educators in West Germany conducted an experiment in self-expression among young children living in three new towns and three older cities. Comparing their paintings and drawings, the researchers found that whereas the city child was stimulated by his environment, the new-town child tended to be unimaginative and bland. They concluded that for the latter, the overplanned character of the surroundings inhibited his natural curiosity and blunted his creativity.

By the year 2000, 80 percent of the American people will live in cities; world-wide, during this time, as many buildings will be erected as have gone up in all recorded history. Most environmentalists agree that the one thing our cities will not be is futuristic —at least in appearance. They are far more likely to be complex and cluttered than simple and orderly, although the clutter will be there with a purpose. Planners are thinking less in terms of efficiency than of the mental image the city projects onto its inhabitants. The new urban aesthetic, some believe, will avoid the traditional lines of scale and perspective in favor of how people go about their daily

business. In brief, cities will probably be built around the behavioral needs of the inhabitants, rather than as monuments to their architects.

If the environmentalists have their way, we will carve up our cities to give residents a greater sense of belonging. Smaller schools and parks, more intimately designed public areas,

promenades to break up the sameness of block layouts, more regard for the unique character of the neighborhoods—all this will help us personalize space.

Nor will institutions be quite as institutional-looking in the future. In Boston, a new pediatrics hospital is being built in a cluster arrangement around open courtyards and "floated" over a shopping plaza. What might have been a threatening superstructure to young patients will be a decentral-

If the environmentalists have their way, we will carve up our cities to give residents a greater sense of belonging. Smaller schools and parks, more intimately designed public areas, promenades to break up the sameness of block layouts, more regard for the unique character of the neighborhoods—all this will help us to personalize our space.

ized complex that's part of a familiar neighborhood. Los Angeles architect C. M. Deasy, in redesigning an obsolescent school in a black area, put a public sidewalk through the grounds as a means of bringing the local community into closer contact with the school, thus giving the citizens a better idea of what's going on behind the fences. As a result, most of the friction between outsiders and the school staff has disappeared. In housing projects, there will be participatory planning like Piero Patri's, with the occupants helping decide the environmental mix.

Can we eliminate the noise of the city? The Federal Council of Scientists reports a doubling of environmental sound level every ten years, and at this rate, the decibels may become lethal. No doubt, legislation will intervene first, but not all noise will go away. Some of the most imaginative planning in sonic design is being done by Michael Southworth, who not merely would fight noise but wants to beat it at its own game. He would use symbolic sounds to inform pedestrians of such things as the weather and approaching buses. Street criers would relay public information; in squares and parks, large, animated sculptures would make sounds when people moved around them; and in ugly areas, sequences of different floor materials would squeak, rumble, squish or pop to provide interest when walked upon. Where there is visual monotony, Southworth says, add new sounds, such as splashing water fountains, bells and boat horns.

Fanciful? Probably, but it indicates one way the psychodesigners are trying to make a world in which we will feel at home. It's not simply the destruction of natural resources we must be concerned with now and in the future; we must also create an environment that can allow us to become more human.

SOME QUESTIONS FOR PROBING:

1. WHAT DOES YOUR APARTMENT/HOME REVEAL ABOUT YOUR OWN LIFE-STYLE?

2. HOW MIGHT YOU INFLUENCE SOMEONE'S BEHAVIOR BY USING FURNITURE CHANGE OR PLACEMENT?

3. HAVE YOU EVER SEEN NOISE INFLUENCE SOMEONE'S BEHAVIOR?

4. WHAT ARE YOUR OWN RESPONSES TO BEING CROWDED?

5. CAN LANDSCAPING BE USED AS A MESSAGE? HOW?

6. IN YOUR TOWN, WHAT DO YOUR URBAN LIGHTING PATTERNS TELL YOU?

7. WHAT KIND OF ENVIRONMENT BORES YOU? EXCITES YOU? CALMS YOU?

8. DOES COLOR MAKE A DIFFERENCE IN YOUR RESPONSE TO ENVIRONMENT?

9. DO YOU RESPOND DIFFERENTLY TO ROUGH TEXTURES THAN TO SMOOTH ONES? SOFT TEXTURES VERSUS HARD ONES?

10. IN YOUR USUAL HOME ENVIRONMENT, WHAT VARIABLES CAN YOU MANIPULATE THAT WOULD MAKE A DIFFERENCE IN THE WAY PEOPLE FELT THERE?

11. HAVE YOU EVER EXPERIENCED COMMERCIAL PLACES (RESTAURANTS, BARS, PUBLIC BUILDINGS, ETC.) DELIBER-ATELY STRUCTURING THE ENVIRONMENT TO AFFECT PEOPLE'S BEHAVIOR? WHERE . . . AND HOW?

12. WHAT IS NECESSARY IN YOUR ENVIRONMENT FOR YOU TO EXPERIENCE "PRIVACY"? DO YOU HAVE PRIVACY IF YOU CAN BE SEEN? HEARD? TOUCHED? SMELLED?

13. WHAT CAUSES YOU TO PAY ATTENTION TO CERTAIN SIGNS AND ADVERTISEMENTS, WHILE IGNORING OTHERS?

After reading the previous articles, is there any doubt in your mind that word-communication is but a small part of our total symbol exchange?

I have always been impressed with the complex and intricate wonder of a child learning to speak. Yet my awe is even greater as I think about the unconscious learning of several *nonverbal* vocabularies. It is not an exaggeration to say that we are brilliant and creative creatures—to accomplish such a feat.

Unconscious masters of nonverbal communication.

The path to balanced communication is to *surface* our awareness, to make conscious what is now below our threshold of awareness. Consider how often you rely on traffic signals, clothing and cosmetic

142 cues, clocks and whistles, rumbles from the stomach, coolness or warmth of the skin, and color cues to tell the salt from the pepper. And most of this without thought.

We must become as aware of our silent language as we are of our spoken language. Both ends of the spectrum must be respected.

To come to a centered position.

And this awareness begins with questions.

6

Being
Centered

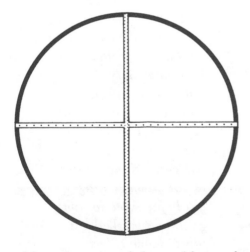

The Sioux Indians have a symbol for their view of existence. It is a circle, a wooden hoop, which represents all things— the whole of reality. Stretched across the circle are two strips of rawhide. One is red. The other is black.

The red north-south line (up and down on this page) stands for the path of spiritual development. The black east-west line (side to side) represents earthly existence and the problems of normal living.

144   Where the two lines cross at center is a holy state.

It is YOU.

Your life experience at this time. Your journey through life. Your place on the scale of spiritual development. The living of your life in its present balance of physical and spiritual dimensions.

To me, this Indian symbol for centered, holy living is an echo of the mandalas of Christian, Buddhist, Hindu, and Islam perceptions.

Its place in this book is basic, because COMMUNICATION BEHAVIOR, LIKE ALL OTHER BEHAVIOR, IS A REFLECTION AND FUNCTION OF PERSONAL BALANCE.

Balanced communication flows from center to center.

If you would significantly change behavior, look to its origin, its source, its seed-place. Or, as Bernard Gunther says it:

a man leaving town
one early morning
was stopped and asked
by an old wise man
where he was going
out to save this mess
of a world was his reply
oh said the wise man
tell me how things are
in this country
terrible was the reply
there's graft and corruption
and incompetence everywhere
and how about in your village
asked the old one
it's a huge muddle he said
no one knows what they're doing
just a lot of graft and greed
and in your household

asked the knowing one
miserable replied the fellow
there's always fighting
selfishness and jealousy
and within yourself
asked the wonderous one
turmoil replied the traveller
confusion conflict
tension anxiety
not a moment's peace
look said the seeing one
before you go out
to save the world
straighten things out
in your own country
but before you do that
get things worked out
in your own village
and take care of the

situation within your family
but before you try to get
those things straight

get into harmony
with your own being

then perhaps when you
get things balanced
within yourself
you can help straighten
out your family

and then you can worry
about lending a hand
in your village
and when you've got
things worked out
in your village
perhaps then you can
help get your country
in shape and
when your country is
in good condition
then go out and
save the world

If you would achieve balanced communication, achieve balanced living. Without internal center, there can be no external balance. As I watch children I am reminded of this. My son Kahlil provides an analogy that might make the point. He is learning to walk. It is a new task for him, and one at which he apparently has no experience, yet he seems to know exactly what must be done and how to go about it. He never exceeds his limits, and his sense of physical balance is incredible. When he sits on the floor his back is straight, head balanced, and crossed legs knee-touch the ground. He is solid, relaxed, centered. And he's teaching me a lot.

I suspect most children have similar messages to communicate.

i wish
i could remember
what i knew
when i was five
i think i had
the answer
then
having just
recently arrived

i recall
that i could
change into
a dragonfly
and when
you know
how to do this
you know everything

no wonder
i
cried
when they
sent me off
on that
first
day
of
school

RIC MASTEN

It is my belief that adults, too, can affirm/reaffirm contact with center. We have learned to look away; we can learn to see through. We can *unlearn* our lack of knowledge.

For example, consider the life energy many people waste on personal "problems." Many souls have learned the unknowledge of *worry:* they expend their energy without changing their situation. Worrying requires that people remain CONFUSED, and that means using a great deal of energy to avoid seeing, avoid listening, avoid thinking, and avoid acting. This existential avoidance—confusion—demands intense psychic and physical energy, for no apparent benefit. Yet this off-center, self-generated anxiety state is created daily by millions of adults.

KNOW ANYONE LIKE THIS?

Another variation on the same theme: people who have learned the unknowledge that "problems" are due to the "outside world." They do not understand that problems are frustrated goals. They do not perceive that *they* determine those goals; *they* assign priorities of achievement; *they* limit the means used to reach their goals; *they* control the amount of energy used to achieve; and *they* set the timetable. In addition, *they* determine when and how frustration will be the response *they* make in the situation *they* have created. Yet this off-balance waste of life energy is common.

EVER SEEN SUCH BEHAVIOR?

The point is that we do not *have to* embrace toxic unknowledge, even though it is the normal and current brand of superstition.

But let's be honest about this.

It isn't just a question of *knowing,* is it?

To me, it is also a question of how I *act* on what I know.

My awareness must translate into behavior, if my life is to be what I wish it to be. My daily *behavior* is the key to my success in life. It's not what I know, but what I *do* that gets results.

For example, did you hear of the English housewife who weighed 238 pounds, and claimed that she wanted to stop eating "but just couldn't"? She knew the problems this weight caused for her health, and she was troubled because she couldn't wear fashionable clothes. But she wouldn't *act* to change the situation. Her distress was not caused by lack of awareness, but by lack of appropriate behavior.

Finally she couldn't stand herself that way any longer . . . and she acted. She arranged for a surgical operation in which her jaws and teeth were cemented together—so she couldn't eat! And she lost weight in a hurry. During her self-imposed lockjaw, Mrs. Turner (of Carlton, England) subsisted on tea, coffee, and tomato soup spiced with vinegar.

You might guess what happened as soon as she regained use of her mouth. Her dieting action was not "appropriate," because it did not deal with her basic unwillingness to stop eating so much. And eating is a behavior, not an awareness.

So people can remain off-center through lack of proper action, as well as through lack of knowledge.

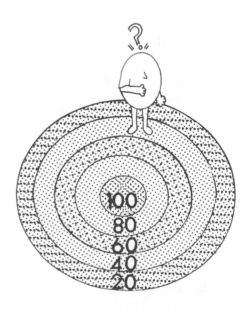

You can tell, I'm sure, that I strongly believe that Man (myself, for example) has as many options as he cares to perceive.

Man has choice about his level of awareness.

And about how he behaves.

Yes, it's true I've spent years being conditioned to certain ways of thinking and behaving in my culture; I share the framework of perceptions and behaviors that stamps me as "American." I do have habits of behavior. Long learned. Deeply ingrained and easily stimulated.

In fact, *most* of my daily behavior is made up of responses learned
long ago (self-programmed). The way I wash, eat, speak, hold my body
when I walk or run, read, smile, drive, even do the dishes. And I admit
that if I had to remain sensitive and open to the newness of every daily
situation I would be exhausted very quickly. It is a positive virtue of
my habits that they save me energy and the need to rethink each
separate perception and behavior throughout the day.

BUT . . . this does *not* mean that I have no control over my life.

For instance, suppose that I am in a situation in which I am afraid
of someone or something. My heart may be lickity-splitting away, my
lungs pumping rapidly, my imagination running wild. I am *still* in
charge of the decision as to how I translate this response into overt
behavior. I need not remain locked-in to old habits of fear response,
such as avoidance or attack. I am not limited to these two alternatives,
just because I have learned them in the past (and in some situations
found them useful).

I have the option of   ELABORATING

or

CHANGING

or

ELIMINATING present habits.

Therefore, when I experience dissatisfaction, frustration, and confusion
in my life, I have the choice of changing or discontinuing unsuccessful
behaviors or viewpoints, to change the outcome of currently unreward-
ing situations.

After all, dissatisfaction, frustration, and confusion are all self-
created conditions. Self-created conditions. Self-created conditions.

CAN YOU THINK OF A SINGLE EXCEPTION TO THIS
STATEMENT?

I create my own goals . . .
expectations . . .
behavior . . .
world.

A lonely person is one who avoids genuine contact.

An angry person is one who angers.

A loving person is one who loves.

A thoughtful person is one who thinks.

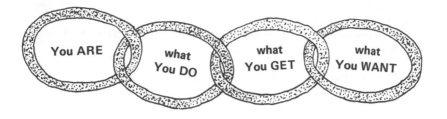

My guess is that you agree that you have choice in life, or you wouldn't be reading this book. So let's swing back to the central question of this chapter. The question of being centered.

WHAT IS AT THE CENTER OF YOUR WORLD?

On what awareness do you base your living actions? On what foundation of values or needs or perceptions do you decide your life-style? What is your touchstone of being?

It seems reasonable that if my behavior is not related to fulfilling my most personal vision of human be-ing, then I am far from centered, far from balanced. If my daily life has strayed from what I know to be true, from what I most intimately value, then why am I going on? What am I doing?

Psychologist Abraham Maslow believes that there is a universal scale of human values that applies to all of us. And he suggests that there are levels or priorities of values, or "needs." Only after a lower level value has been fulfilled does a man focus or move on to fulfill the next most important.

SELF-ACTUALIZATION

BE ALL THAT ONE IS

DEVELOP HIGHEST
POTENTIALS

GIVE LOVE AND RESPECT

SELF-ESTEEM

RESPECT FROM SELF

RESPECT FROM OTHERS

LOVE AND BELONGINGNESS

BELONG

BE ACCEPTED

BE LOVED

HAVE FRIENDS

SAFETY AND SECURITY

CLOTHING

SHELTER

PROTECTION FROM
THE ENVIRONMENT

BASIC PHYSICAL STATE

FOOD

WATER

SLEEP

While this priority order is not absolute, Maslow says that most of a person's energy will be locked into only one or two levels at a time. According to this perception, we should not expect to see a man worrying about his social status if his belly is empty. He will be seeking food and water, and valuing survival.

DOES THIS FIT YOUR LIFE EXPERIENCE AS TRUE?

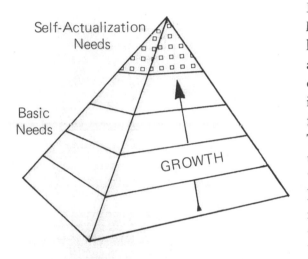

Equally provocative is Maslow's assertion that human be-ing, or self-actualization, can occur only as individuals have fulfilled their basic needs. Then they may move to satisfy their "growth needs" (top level of the pyramid of needs). He feels that this movement from basic to growth needs is the purpose of human life and the direction of human evolution. I am reminded of Carl Rogers's comment that a person who is in touch with his own internal center acts in ways which enhance not only his life, but the lives of those around him.

To hear the silence of my innermost being, I must calm the distracting noise from my fears of failure to survive in the "outer" world.

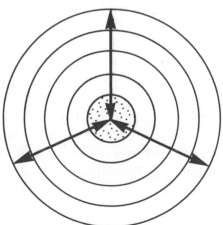

For those of us so caught up in our own routine that we hear nothing but the roar of reflex, behavioral scientist Harold Lasswell has given much thought to this question, and points a direction we might pursue for greater focus.

He believes that a "value" is the preferred outcome of an event. That is, what I want to happen or occur.

I value what I want to happen in the real world.

This fits nicely with Maslow's idea that "needs" and "values" are the same thing. With Lasswell's view on values, now I put the two definitions together and I can say that when I act in a certain way, I do so because I expect fulfillment of a particular need. I am valuing that outcome, that event, that satisfaction. For example, when I am working in my backyard garden I am valuing my physical health as the preferred outcome of the activity.

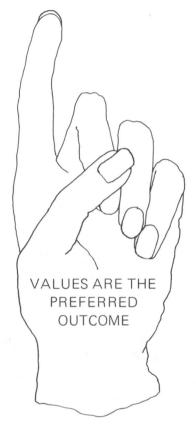

VALUES ARE THE
PREFERRED
OUTCOME

In forming his definition of values, Lasswell traveled to many countries. He kept his eyes open, talked with people from all walks of life, and, upon returning to the United States and thinking about what he had heard and seen, he concluded that HUMAN BEINGS VALUE THE SAME THINGS, REGARDLESS OF THEIR CULTURAL DIFFERENCES!

They may BEHAVE differently to achieve the same value outcomes, and they may vary in the emphasis they place on particular values. But their "preferred outcomes" all fit within eight basic value categories.

Think about your daily behavior for a minute.
See if you discover a behavior you *can't* categorize below.
Try to find a flaw in this classification system. Try to "break" the assertion that:

ALL HUMAN BEHAVIOR EXPRESSES ONE OR MORE OF THESE VALUE CATEGORIES.

1. **AFFECTION.** The degree of love and congenial feelings among people.

2. **RESPECT.** The degree of recognition given to people in their capacity as human beings.

3. **SKILL.** Development of potential talents for their *own* sake, not to achieve some other value.

4. **ENLIGHTENMENT.** The knowledge/information necessary to make important decisions.

5. **POWER.** Participation in making important decisions.

6. **WEALTH.** Possession or claim on both goods *and* services.

7. **FAIRNESS.** Moral or ethical standards and their practice.

8. **WELL-BEING.** Mental and physical health.

If you use this framework to understand your own valuing behavior, there are a few common pitfalls you should avoid.

First, don't mistake a "tool" behavior for the final, desired outcome or value. For example, if you saw me typing this page, you might conclude that I was exhibiting behavior valuing *wealth* . . . since this book will be sold for money. But notice how your interpretation would change if you later discover that I have donated the money to a charity. What was I valuing by typing? Another example comes from my dog's

behavior. Have you ever seen a pet engage in affection behavior, when what he/she really wanted was to be let out at night? So hang loose on your observations. Don't mistake the tool for the value. It's easy to do when you look at others' behaviors.

Second, be aware that interpreting the behavior of *others* is a very risky business. By that I mean that it is difficult to tell what others are valuing by their external behavior. When you look at the young executive who works sixteen hours a day, be careful about concluding that he/she is valuing WEALTH by that behavior. If you talk with the young executive's secretary, you might learn that the person is supporting a younger brother through medical school, thereby valuing AFFECTION. Or if you hang around the water cooler you might learn that our young executive desires to impress the firm's president. And that's a very different valuing going on.

Third, know that you may "share" a value, or "deny" a value with/to someone else. I might *share* the value of RESPECT, for example, by quietly listening to my four-year-old daughter Paulyn explain her trip to the beach. I might *deny* her the value of RESPECT by snubbing her attempts to communicate, and refusing to recognize the importance of her desire or her experience.

CAN YOU THINK OF WHEN SOMEONE DENIED YOU A VALUE?

HOW ABOUT AN EXAMPLE OF SOMEONE SHARING A VALUE WITH YOU?

Naturally, considering something as basic as your value structure may bring to mind those two frauds of human existence known as "good" and "bad." These judgment words come to mind almost automatically, and I urge you to resist their influence. They often reflect self-programmed tapes made years ago, and readily distort your clear vision.

In this regard, I would like to share with you two meditation techniques that help me get beyond that kind of programming in my own thinking. The first employs the yin-yang concept of which I spoke earlier in the book.

You'll recall that yin-yang is a viewpoint that expresses all life as a polarity. Within the whole (represented by the circle) are the equal elements of evil-good, active-passive, young-old, and so on. Notice that the symbol also suggests that in all white there is some black, in all male there is some female . . . and vice versa.

Here the meditation involves me in seeking full understanding of each of the opposite poles, and of similarities between them.

Try it yourself.

Consider the Tao

Take a particularly "negative" situation in your present life, and deliberately explore and elaborate on the "positive" pole. For instance, suppose that you are without money. Flat broke. Out of bread. Meditate on the positive benefits of being broke.

What can you *learn* while broke, that is not available when you have a fat bank account? What *new experiences* become available? What *growth* opportunities exist? What happens to your *values* now? How are you becoming more/less *tolerant*? What *new competencies* develop as a result of the situation? What have you gained by being broke that you did not have before?

I'm not speaking of ignoring the "negative" element of your situation. Simply of understanding and exploring the opposite.

Now take a particularly "positive" situation in your present life, and run the same number on it . . . clarifying the "negative" balance.

Although difficult at first, because you are not used to exploring in this way, you will soon find this way of thinking easier and much more profitable than the "normal" one-sided judgment of life. My experience has been that I am more able to flow with and capitalize on situations. I realize that *every* action is a positive experience; every "enemy" is a potential friend; every human relationship is an opportunity to grow.

There is no way to lose. Everything is gain!

The second meditation builds upon the first, utilizing the yin-yang perception, then moving beyond. This teaching originated in Japan by a man named Susumu Ijiri, and echoes the ancient *Chinese Book of Changes* (*I Ching*). There is no name for this method of thinking, but since it is done with a pillow it might be called pillow education.

A pillow has four sides and a middle. Any problem has four approaches and a middle. In this exercise you move around each of the four sides of a pillow and back to the middle, placing your hands at each point as you consider each approach to your situation. By the time you finish, you will have taken a total of five different views of your problem.

I actually have a "problem pillow" at home which I use, but any old pillow will do. In fact, there is no real reason why you need use a pillow. It is only a convenient analogy and marker of your progress as you go from one point of view to another.

Let me move around the pillow once, to demonstrate how this works. And in this example, let's suppose that I am concerned about

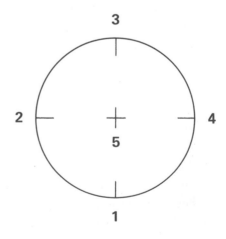

writing well. Perhaps the preliminary reviews of this book have indicated that I am not expressing myself clearly; or perhaps my publisher feels my writing sounds "too academic." At any rate, I am having doubts about my writing.

I sit before my pillow and place my hands at the number one position. My position here is: "I am not writing well." A flat statement, trimmed of fat and fancy. Once I have this position clearly stated, I let my imagination roam over all of the implications of this position. I fantasize the imaginary horribles of not writing well; I really get into

being a not-o.k. writer. How does my writing look in this condition? How do people react? How do I feel? How will my life be affected because of this terrible truth? And I also keep in mind that this is only my NOW position; it is possible that it may sometimes change, since most things do.

Now I move my hands to the number two position. Here I reverse my previous state: "I *am* writing well." This, too, is a direct statement. And here, too, I mentally seek out the corners of this position. How do people react now? How do I feel? How will my life be influenced because I write well? What is the character of my writing?

Like the first position, this reality is part of the whole pillow and equally far from center. It is justified and necessary to the whole of things.

Moving now to position three, I find myself in the condition of both writing well and not writing well. Here is the coexistence of positions one and two . . . at the same time and in the same space. Again my imagination caresses the possibilities. How does it feel to be both? What is the impact on my life? How do others respond? And so on.

Most Americans can understand the first two positions easily; they represent the either-or, black-white, sinner-saint type of thinking. If you're not *for* me, then you're *against* me. You either *are* or *are not* a real man/woman. Such limitation in perception can be observed daily when we pick up a newspaper or listen to a television newscast.

But position three stretches such minds.

Let me ask you . . . is position three not as close to truth as either of the other two? As you examine your life, consider your problems, is not position three justified and of merit?

"You say you are right, husband, and our neighbor is wrong," says the wife to her husband, who is involved in a dispute over property. "But may there not also be a place where you are wrong and he is right? And both of you may be wrong and both right. Isn't this true?"

I conclude my consideration of position three by observing that it is a necessary part of the whole, equally far from the center as any other of the sides. And therefore of merit.

The meditation continues.

I move to position number four. Here it is that I am *neither* writing well, *nor* am I not writing well. It is here I seek understanding of how I am when neither of the poles exists for me. When I surpass considera-

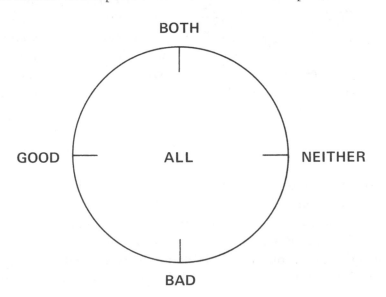

tion of this as an issue in my life. When such attention is pointless and forgotten. And this position, too, is a necessary part of the whole, and equally far from the center of things. Hence, of merit.

As I conclude, I cup both hands in the middle of my pillow, which affirms the nameless center from which all positions emerge. This center place represents the originative harmony from which all changing conditions stem, says Mr. Ijiri. And before its importance in awareness, all other positions fade.

My final gesture is to place my hands once again at each of the four positions, while affirming to myself that each is good and necessary to the whole.

In his book *Square Sun, Square Moon*, Paul Reps comments that the Japanese children from whom he learned this exercise do not count with numbers. They have names for the four positions and center, which are a Japanese five-steps-into-universal-harmony of ancient and unknown origin. Those names are *Hi, Ri, Ho, Ken,* and *Ten.*

Whether you use these names or just numbers, however, you will find that this contemplation exercise will tend to "open up" your view of what is before you.

My only claim for these meditations is that they help *me* to maintain a more balanced, more accurate view of my life situations. I don't succumb as easily anymore to the labeling behavior of "good" or "bad," and I find my center place more readily without such distractions taken meaningfully.

Whether or not you will benefit from these exercises I don't know. But I am aware that there are no quick-and-easy, instant-insight formulas available—that work. I should know that, because I've tried almost all I've ever heard of. Even the drug scene, which some people advocate as a short-cut to self-awareness, only lets you down again after the high. And if by rare chance some chemical stimulus *does* help you achieve a degree of self-insight, you still face the problem of being without tools-to-change when you get back on the ground. For it's down here we spend most of our time.

For me, at this point in my life, I am convinced that centered living requires of me balance in every aspect of my life.

The food I eat.	Social relationships.
My body exercise.	The emotions I generate.
Mental development.	My use of resources/energy.

And most importantly

My SPIRITUAL growth.

I know. I know. There are some people who think that mention of "spiritual growth" is out of place in a book of this kind. But I believe them to be shortsighted rather than insighted.

Without *felt* consciousness of this dimension I would be stunted. Without a sure grounding in moral truth, as best I can discern it, my actions and my life are reactive rather than proactive. If you will, call such grounding "value orientation" or my "view of life," since the word "spiritual" is disquieting to some. But don't disregard my basic point: FROM MORAL CENTER FLOWS THE ENERGY OF DAILY ACTION.

The price of forgetting this may be witnessed in the corruption of our daily existence. Political. Military. Commercial. Educational. Family. Religious. Medical. Artistic. Thousands upon millions of decisions and actions without reference to center.

A complex jumble of communications without a thread back home.
And the result is a lack of quality in life. A lack of zest.
Which need not be.

We are precious living seeds. Every one of us.

Eggs of evolution

With CHOICE.

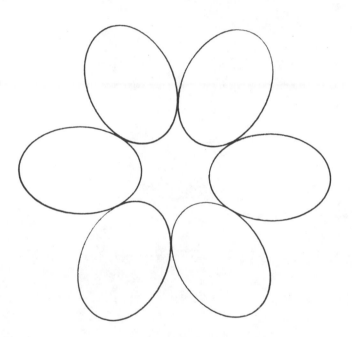

Commune

Community

Communicate